THE RAGAMUFFIN

The Rory McClelland Story

Rory McClelland

Published by Rory McClelland in 2025

Copyright © Rory McClelland, 2025

Rory McClelland has asserted his right to be identified as the author of this work.

All rights reserved. No part of this publication may be reproduced, stored in any retrieval system, or transmitted, in any form or by any means, electronic, mechanical, photocopying, recording or otherwise, without the prior written permission of the publishers.

Book ISBN: 9798307977200

Dedicated to the memory of my son, Rory McClelland

Chapter 1
Ma, Da & the Other Twenty-One

I was my mother's twenty-first child, but not her last. That was my little sister Margaret, who was born a year later. To tell the truth, I struggle to name them all today. Starting with the youngest, there was Margaret, me, Martha (my favourite), Anne, Ali (Alan), Fudgie (Herbert), Gerry, Desser (Desmond – also known The Wizard), Bernadette (The Wizard's twin), Mayme, Matt, Lily, Paddy, Frank and Joe.

I couldn't name the ones who didn't survive. There were three sets of twins, as far as I can remember. My mother christened me Rowland, which only goes to show that she was running out of names. I never liked Rowland. It was too much of a mouthful, so over time, it became Rory. Ma only ever called me Rowland, though she often shortened it to Roll, or Rolly – especially if she wanted me to do something.

My second name was also a bit of a mouthful I suppose. McClelland. Most people get it wrong. My father's father was a Scotsman. He was in the merchant navy, and met my granny – who I never knew – in Cork. But they got sense and moved to Dublin.

Da was the manager of the Nugget Boot Polish factory – a famous landmark in Bluebell back in the day. That's where we were from. Bluebell. Today it's a suburb a few miles south west of the city centre, but back then it was barely a village and Dublin was a long way off. I was born in 1941, a year into The Emergency – which was what World War II was called in Ireland. At that time we lived in what was called a Nugget house, in that it was owned by the factory. We called it 'The Yellow House'. The river Camac ran at the bottom of the garden. This made the house damp, and had a terrible effect on my mother's lungs. She suffered badly from asthma all her life. That's why we upped sticks and moved in with her sister and her family at the other end of the village. We thought we were crowded before! You can imagine the noise in that house.

Soon after that, the British army gave us a house in Camac Park, one of thirty-two houses built for ex-soldiers: men, like my father, Patrick McClelland, who had survived World War I. He had distinguished himself on the battlefield, but I never learned the details. Like most of the men who came back from that terrible war, he never wanted to talk about it. My mother always said that he had saved many lives, and was mentioned in dispatches. She said too that he'd got a letter from the king commending him for his valour, but I never saw this letter.

His heroism earned him a promotion to sergeant, but soon after that, he was captured and held in a huge prisoner of war camp in India. There, he became known as 'The Tattooed Sergeant' because on his back, he had the crucifix with the two robbers on either side. In these camps, you didn't have much to do, so everyone got tattoos. There was only one colour ink available, so you could have any tattoo you wanted so long as it was blue. Da was later promoted to colonel and put in charge of the whole place.

Because of his reluctance to talk about his experiences, I learned most of the story from my uncle Joe, years after my father had died.

'I idolised your da,' Joe told me, 'I was always following him around.' I can imagine him, trailing after his older brother, and the older brother getting annoyed and telling him to go on home for himself. After my da left to sign up with the army, Joe followed him up to Belfast and joined the same regiment, and ended up in the same prisoner of war camp. This was enormous – there were thousands of prisoners there. Joe spent weeks looking for his brother. He'd stop people and ask them, 'Do you know the tattooed sergeant?'

Eventually, he found someone who said, 'I do but he's not a sergeant anymore, he's a colonel. There's his tent there.'

So Joe walked into the tent. My da had his back to him, so Joe says, 'Howaya Patsy!'

My da spun round. 'You! You little bastard! You're still following me!'

Da didn't even know that Joe had signed up, and here he was in the same tent in the same camp thousands of miles from home. Da hit him a belt but then of course he gave him a hug.

Despite the fact that my father got himself a good job when he got home, we always struggled, simply because there were so many mouths to feed. I remember us all heading off to mass on Christmas morning. We were like a little army marching down the street. When we got there, we took up two pews on our own.

Back then, everyone had big gardens so you could grow your own vegetables. Da also had a plot up beside the factory, which was only a hundred yards away. He grew spuds there, and that's what we lived on. We'd get through two stone of them a day. That's nearly thirteen kilograms.

I was a bit delicate. I remember my mother often bringing me for chest X-Rays to Steeven's Hospital down beside Heuston Station. It's the HQ of the HSE now. Of course, she wasn't that well herself. When the asthma got bad, she had this device she'd put on. It had a big mask that went over her face, with a well at the centre which held something that helped her to breathe, and there was a big bulb on the end that you squeezed to give you a puff.

Most of us younger ones slept upstairs, spread between three beds in the one room. The house had a very high pitched roof – it's still standing – and we were all crowded in there under the eaves. Sometimes Ma would sleep up there too. She used to sit up in the bed and call out each of our names in turn. Everyone would let on to be asleep. But I hadn't the heart to do that, so when she'd call: 'Roll?' I'd say 'Yes Ma'.

'Would you make your Mammy a cup of tea?'

I'd get up and go downstairs, wearing only the little shift I had for bed. The tiles were freezing cold under my feet. I'd make the tea and bring it up to her.

It was always a struggle for Ma, but when I was making my First Holy Communion, she managed to find me a suit – God only knows where or how. I was as proud as punch in that suit, which had a lovely little rosette at the lapel. She sent me round to the neighbours so everyone would have the privilege of seeing me in my finery.

At one house, the woman said, 'Tell your mammy you're lovely.'

'She knows!' I said.

I got slagging over that for years afterwards.

None of us ever gave Ma any cheek. You wouldn't dare. She was a country woman – from Westmeath. I remember her listening to

Gaelic football matches on the radio when Westmeath would be playing. I'd say 'Come on Dublin!' and run like hell.

We went off down to visit her sisters an odd time. I used to love that. I remember them collecting haycocks from the fields. They had a dray: a cart with a steel floor, and the back of it used to tilt down to touch the ground. Then they'd put ropes around the haycocks and pull them up one by one.

There were orchards too. They only had crab apples but we'd eat them anyway. I remember I was fighting one of my cousins in my auntie's house, and she came along, grabbed the two of us and flung us out the door and down the steps.

She had another sister married in Drimnagh: Emily. She was very good to us, and we were very close to her family. If my mother was unwell or if anything went wrong, it was 'Send for Emmie'. She'd come over, take charge and make sure we were all alright. We all felt safe when she was around. We were all so afraid of my mother dying.

I adored my da and my ma, but I was mostly my da's boy. He was getting old by this time but of course I didn't see that. He used to get all dolled up on a Sunday morning and go down to the Workman's Club in Inchicore for a couple of pints or to play a game of billiards, and then he'd come home and himself and my ma would go off to bed for the afternoon. My sister would get in beside my mother and I'd get in beside my Dad.

    He used to do this amazing trick. He'd take out his handkerchief, then reach into his inside pocket, and moving his hand under the hanky, he'd make it look as if he was holding a baby rabbit. Coming up with these sorts of tricks was how they used to amuse themselves in the prison camp. Not that there was much to do in our house at night either. We used to have a competition: name all the Paddies around here: there'd be Paddy O'Keefe, Paddy Murphy, Paddy O'Leary ... and so on. When we got tired of that, we'd try to name all the jobs the Wizard had. That's how he got the name; he had an amazing ability to find a job no problem. He was a bit of an oddball. You wouldn't know what he'd come out with. One time he grabbed me by the ankle – I was only eight – spun me around and flung me into the canal. I couldn't swim. I somehow scrambled along the bottom till I got to the side and someone pulled me out. I had a nervous reaction to this experience, and couldn't stop laughing, but this quickly turned into a fit of crying.

Somebody robbed the local shop one time, and this fella told the police my brother did it. We were all in bed when the cops arrived and began banging on the door, demanding to be let in. We all got up and followed Daddy down to the door, crowding around him as he opened it up. One of the cops had a torch which lit up my father's face.

'Get that light out of my eyes now!' Da was standing there in nothing but his nightshirt, but he exuded authority. He had been in charge of thousands of men in that prison camp, and could turn on this tremendous sense of power and gravitas when he needed to.

The copper immediately put the light away. 'Oh sorry!' he said.

Da couldn't stop them from taking my brother away, but he was sent home a short while after that. My brother maintained he didn't do it, and my father believed him, but there was a stain on the house because of the accusation.

We found out afterwards that the cops then went to the house of the man who squealed on my brother and knocked on his door. There was no answer, but as they were leaving, one of them saw the curtain twitch, so they went back and found all the stuff that had been stolen inside. It was a great relief to us all when my brother was exonerated.

But I was always terrified of coppers and what they might do. There was one time, I was coming down the road when I saw one of my brothers coming out of a garden with a bunch of his mates, all laden down with stolen apples. Next thing, a copper comes pedalling up the street towards them and the lads legged it. Most of them made it to this room below the local shop – there was a stairs down from the street. I followed them, like an eejit, and hid there in the half darkness. My heart nearly left my body when I heard the heavy tread and saw those big black boots and the blue serge trousers come down those steps. There was no escape, so we all stood up among the apples now scattered around the floor. My brother told me to go home, that I hadn't anything to do with it but the copper gave him a punch into the head. 'I give the orders around here.'

He took my brother off, and I went home, bawling crying. I cannot for the life of me remember what happened after that, but I suppose he got off with a warning.

I started school when I was about six. St. Cillian's in Robinhood, which was about half a mile away. Everyone there seemed to have a bit more money than we did, but I suppose that wouldn't be difficult. We had three teachers: the two Misses Cooney and Miss Maher. Biddy Cooney was one of the most terrifying women I've ever known. Even thinking about her now is after putting my stomach in knots. I remember her screaming at the top of her lungs. The fear it would put in you! I can still taste it. I remember her swinging a girl around by the hair. It was a terrible thing to look at. Schools could be very violent places back then of course. Biddy's sister Sheila was not a very nice person either, but Miss Maher? Ah, Miss Maher was lovely.

I remember one day, not long after I'd started, I arrived into school with no shoes on.

She must have noticed this at some point because she announced that we'd be having a dancing lesson, and that everyone had to take off their shoes. This was unusual; we'd never had a dancing lesson before. When we finished, she said, 'You can sit down now, and if you want to leave off your shoes, you can leave off your shoes.'

She had engineered the whole thing for me. If anyone noticed I had no shoes, they'd assume it was because I hadn't put them on again after the dancing. Otherwise they might well have given me a hard time over it.

This wasn't the end of her kindness either. At lunchtime, she went off to her lunch – something she didn't usually do. A while later, she stuck her head around the door so that only I could see her, and she signalled to me to come out into the hall. She had a bag full of clothes.

'Here,' she said, 'take this home and tell no one only your mammy where you got them.'

School hadn't finished for the day, but again, she didn't want her act of charity noticed. Children can be cruel, and if they got a sniff of the fact that we were as needy as we were, they wouldn't have been shy about letting me know.

Years later, when I came home from England with money in my pocket, I went into town and bought a big bunch of flowers for that woman, but I just couldn't find the courage to go and give them to her. I regret that to this day.

We were worried about my Ma dying, but it was my da we should have been bothered about. When I was eight or nine, he started going into hospital regularly. I didn't pay this too much attention, I had no idea that there was anything seriously wrong with him, even when I used to visit him in hospital. I remember those visits very clearly. The hospital was so big and so *clean*; afterwards, walking home, you'd have that lovely smell of Dettol on your clothes. But those visits were all about my da. I idolised that man. It was a treat just to be able to hold his hand. He was kind and gentle, but firm. He never had to shout. I didn't think anything could happen to him. Maybe I was living in hope. I was only nine years old.

I was playing outside one Saturday morning when I saw this woman hurrying up the road towards our house. She lived about a mile away, and had one of the only telephones in the area. I watched her turn at our gate and go into our house, and next thing I heard my sister screaming. The hospital had rung to say that my da had died. The bottom dropped out of my world.

Chapter 2
Ragamuffin Days

We were never told what killed him, but we think it was cancer. I suppose too that his years in that Indian prisoner-of-war camp must have taken their toll on his heath.

Another regret: I didn't go to his funeral. My ma said, 'Will you stay with me?' I should have but I didn't, I wanted to be with my cousins, who were going back to their own house. I suppose I was only a child and had no notion of what I wanted.

From then on, the hardship and the hunger were desperate. The company that Da had worked for weren't that good to us at all. My mother got two pound a week pension from them. This helped, but it didn't match the level of responsibility he had. He'd been in charge of the whole place, he used to hold interviews in the house. People would be calling day and night looking for work.

The nights got hungrier and the winters got colder. We had a range in the kitchen – that was the only source of heat in the house, but we couldn't afford to have it on that often.

Myself and my brothers used to go over the fields to the slang, which was this little kind of a wilderness area, and we'd cut the boughs off the trees and bring them home for firewood. We had electricity and we had gas for cooking, but they cost money. You had to put a shilling in the slot to get the power going. A ha'penny would work just as well, but of course when the man came to open up the box, all of these ha'pennies would tumble out. My mother always made up the money one way or another. We might have been poor, but we had respectability. That was very important to her.

There were no indoor toilets of course, and even outside, it wasn't a flush toilet, just a sort of a commode over a hole in the ground in a narrow brick outhouse. The cold in winter! One time I remember I was down on my hunkers over the hole when my sister arrived out with one of her friends and hauled me off it. I went flying, and struggled to get my pants up before her mate saw me willy!

I got older and bolder. I used to rob orchards, or I'd steal a bit of cabbage. I'd rob any food I got the chance to rob and bring it home to my mother. She'd give me a clatter, but she'd always take whatever it was and boil it up. She was a great cook, she made fantastic food and I don't know how she did it. If she had a few rashers, she'd stick the spoon into the mashed spuds and pour the grease from the pan into the hole. It was gorgeous! I had a ferocious appetite when I was growing up and she did her best to fatten me up. I remember one day, she had a few spuds leftover and asked me if I wanted them.

I did.

'Nothing goes waste,' she said, 'when there's a pig around.'

I got upset. 'Don't call me a pig!'

If she had the money, she'd send us down to the local shop to for the bits and pieces that they stocked. This was just another of the Camac Park houses that the owners – the Begleys – turned into a shop. They were Protestants, and lovely people. But Mr. Begley wasn't fond of exercise.

'Mr. Begley, could I have half a pound of butter?'

'You can, but will you wait till someone else comes in Rory?'

He didn't want to get out of the chair until he had a couple of people to serve.

Rationing was still going on up until I was around ten. There were so many of us that the Begleys couldn't give us all the bread we were entitled to, so one of my brothers made a box car, and we used to have to go over to Drimnagh to a shop where my auntie worked to get the bread. But often, even that wasn't enough. Honest to God, some nights you'd be crying with the hunger, but there was nothing Ma could do. She never went out, never spent a penny on herself. She gave it all up for us.

I used to have a recurring dream around this time. I was in a chip shop and I was just after finding a pound. A pound! I'll get fish and chips, I would say to myself. I'd be about to be served and the place would turn into a clothes shop. Then I'd wake up.

Me and my next sister up – Martha – we were the wild ones. She used to come robbing apples with me. One time we were in a neighbour's garden taking what we could grab. Next thing we heard voices, so we escaped over the fence, then over the next fence so that we were three gardens away. We could hear them talking. We knew that there were relations of theirs staying with them from England, and when we heard English accents for the first time, we couldn't stop laughing. We'd never heard anything like it. We were laughing so much that we nearly gave ourselves away, but eventually, they went back into the house, and when they did, we climbed into their garden again and filled our jerseys with apples. We brought them back to our mother, she gave us both a clatter, then she made apple tarts.

Today the window of my fourth floor flat in Ballyfermot looks south over Walkinstown, Drimnagh, Ballymount, Templeogue and the Dublin Mountains. It's houses and cranes and factories and office buildings as far as the eye can see, but back then, there was nothing. It was all countryside. We used to come up here to Ballyfermot to pick blackberries. We were country kids, living in an isolated little backwater where nothing ever happened.

The thirty-two semi-detached houses of Camac Park were built in a sort of a square, with big rambling gardens to the front and side and high hedges all around. If I wanted to call on my mate, Tommy Morgan, I'd go out the front door and whistle. He'd hear me in his house across the way and whistle back. Then we might go off together, rambling through the fields.

There were just two strands of wire at the back of the garden separating us from a field of cows. The farmer lived about a mile away. He'd come along with his three-legged stool and milk the cows right there in the field. He didn't ask me for help, but I started to give it anyway. I'd be like a dog, keeping the cows in. I had no shoes, and my feet would be cut from stones and sticks and things hidden in the grass, so the farmer used to give me thruppence for my efforts. He gave me a lot more unbeknownst to himself. I got used to the cows, and they got used to me. I'd wait till night time, then I'd bring out the big pot my mother used for boiling spuds, I'd climb through the wire, catch a cow and milk it into the pot. Free milk. It was great.

There was one time, I had the pot half-full and the bloody cow put her foot right into it, and of course there's always shite on cows' legs, so I had to throw the milk out.

There was plenty of craic too if you knew where to look for it. One time, me and my mates went to see a film called *The Miami Story*. The main character in it was a gangster boss called Big Tony Brill. Well, my mate Tony was mesmerised by this movie. It more or less changed his life. He started fancying himself a bit of a gangster. At the beginning, this mainly involved throwing money around – paying for people into the pictures and things like that. Oh yes, and we also had to call him Big Tony, after your man in the film.

That winter was bloody freezing, and I was the only one still in short trousers, so I said, 'Fuck this' and robbed a pair of my brother Gerry's trousers, turned them inside out and stitched them up. Then I turned them back out again and had a grand pair of drainpipes.

None of the houses had inside running water at the time. We used to all hang around the pump in the middle of the gravel footpath, where everyone came to get water. There was a gang of us there one Sunday morning when the women were passing by on the way home from mass. There was no church in Walkinstown then. They used to say mass in Drimnagh Castle instead. Anyway, Big Tony's mother passed by, but about twenty yards up the street she stopped, turned around and called Tony. He ran up to her, we watched them exchange a few words, then she went on and Tony came back.

'I'm not to play with you anymore,' he said, 'you're a Teddy Boy.'

This was all on account of the home-made drainpipes. She took one look at them and decided I was a Teddy Boy. Her disapproval was ironic as it turned out, because things didn't go so great for Big Tony afterwards. Him and his posh cousin robbed the bank in Clondalkin. They had guns and fired into the ceiling, but they were caught and got six years each in Mountjoy.

Tony was barely out before he did another robbery. He got caught again and went back to Mountjoy for another year. I worked with him many years later, when we were adults, but he was a beaten man then. Prison had been too much for him. He was only a dreamer.

We had a choral and dramatic society in Bluebell too. It all centred on the Aspro factory. Aspro was the thing back then – it was a pain killer you took no matter what was wrong with you. The factory had a big canteen with a stage in it, and we used to put on simple little shows there. There was one we called 'Going to the Races'. We all dressed up and acted it out. I was the doorman. There was one little guy, I had to refuse him entry, then let on to give him a kick in the arse. The show went great, it was a right laugh, to be in it and to look at it. But the following week, I met the woman whose son I'd thrown out and she went for me.

'How dare you kick my Tommy!'

'It was only a play!' I said.

These little ventures were all run by Mr. Jack Doherty. His son taught us dancing, at a shilling a time. It was worth it if you could afford it, but my mother rarely could.

Then there were the toss schools, which were very popular back then, especially on a Sunday. There was one down on the Watery Lane, where the Kylemore Industrial Estate is now, and another just inside the gate of a field near our house. Fortunes would be made and lost in the course of an hour or two.

The boxman, who was in charge of the whole thing, would take off his belt and swing it around in a circle to give the tosser a bit of room. Then fellas would lay bets with each other. I'd say to you, 'I'll bet you two bob it's heads,' and put the two shillings on the ground. If you took the bet, you'd put down your two bob beside mine. The tosser would either toss a couple of ha'pennies, or a matchbox, or sometimes a 'feck', which was just a bit of timber or something like it. Anytime two heads were thrown, you'd have to pay the boxman a shilling. I remember one time, there was a friend of my brother – Tommy was his name – who was doing really well, but risked everything on a single toss and lost the lot, to the point where he didn't have a shilling for the boxman, who drew back and hit him a vicious punch.

I was only a kid at the time; the violence of the boxman shocked me. I thought to myself, 'When I grow up I'll kill him', because I loved Tommy. He was a milkman, and was very good to our family. When he'd call to the door with the milk, I'd say to him, 'Give us a tilly, Tommy' and he'd pour out a half cup for me. And when my mother was in hospital, he'd call into her with a box of chocolates. He was like another brother to us, but he wasn't a fighting man and he never tried to defend himself against the angry boxman.

Because I was at the tail-end of a large family, several of my brothers and sisters moved out and started their own families when I was still young. My oldest sister, Lily, who would become like a second mother to me, got married, and because she and her husband had no place else to go, they moved into the parlour in Camac Park. Lily's husband wasn't the best, but he wasn't the worst either. Sometimes he'd work and sometimes he wouldn't. He was handy, but he was a divil for the drink.

Then they started to have kids. There wasn't room to swing a cat, but we loved those kids. They weren't her kids, they were ours. To this day, Lily's family call my mother Mammy and their own mother, Mam. We were all that close.

We weren't living in the poorest part of Dublin; I think it's fair to say that a lot of the houses around us had a bit more than we had, but because there were so many of us, and because there was so little coming in, my mother found it very difficult to keep clothes on our backs. Alan was the brother nearest in age to me, but he was physically bigger, which meant I didn't even get proper hand-medowns. The kids on the street weren't very kind when there'd be no arse in my trousers, and that used to get to me like nothing else. It made me tough to be honest. I'd hit them, just to get them to stop.

One incident in particular had a very profound effect on me. I was palling with this young fella whose da was a racing-car driver of all things. My own father wasn't long dead at this stage. These people had a big house and a garden with walls all around it. The young fella was going in to his dinner. I had no dinner to go home to, so your man says, 'You wait here for me till I'm finished.' There was a flowerbed with a little kerb around it. I sat down here to wait. Next thing his da walked through the gate. He took one look at me then turned his head away, as if I was a lump of dirt. When the kid came out again, he said to me, 'My da said, "who's that ragamuffin?"'

Ragamuffin. That struck me at the heart. I swore nobody would call me a ragamuffin when I grew up. It gave me a bit of a complex to be honest. I got real touchy about it. And that's why, from the minute I could afford it, I always dressed well.

Because I was so bothered by what people might say to me about my clothes, I'd walk over to the Long Mile Road to find people to pal round with. Nobody jeered me over there because these were poor people out of Corporation houses. I made a lot of friends from all kinds of backgrounds, we all played together and had great fun. I never had any trouble.

We ran wild back then. You could go anywhere. Myself and my mate got poles for vaulting. We put two posts up, with a bar across, ran and jumped over them. It felt like we were sailing high into the sky, but sure it was probably no more than a few feet.

The river Camac ran past the paper mill, which would discharge this foul-smelling pulp into the river. Rotten stuff that could be two inches thick. I tried to jump the river using my pole, but of course it stuck in riverbed and down I went into the slime. Awful. So I went home, got a clatter and then got cleaned up. I was about twelve at the time.

We used to catch the boats going up the canal. They'd be full of barrels of porter coming from Guinness's. We'd climb up on top of these – the fellas driving the boats never minded. And we swam in the canal all the time. There were these hills running along the bank, and you'd get undressed behind them. One of the lads – Larry – lived a few doors up from me. A very nice fella; he use to pal with my brother Alan. One day, we were getting stripped, and he took a run and jumped into the canal, but he'd forgotten he still had his shirt on. He'd a very strict mother and got into serious trouble with her over that. He also had an older brother who was a bit of a snob. Larry was having a cigarette outside the picture house one night and he saw the brother coming up the road, so he tapped the cigarette in a hurry and put it in his pocket, but the butt wasn't out and didn't the suit go on fire. He got into more trouble for that.

We used to play handball up against the wall of the shops in Walkinstown. I remember I was playing this Traveller. He was a lovely fella – Laurence Ward was his name – but he used to play handball with a closed fist. He missed the ball one time and hit me full in the face. I saw stars for the first time in my life. But I shook my head and I was alright.

You'd get into fights from time to time too. It was unavoidable really. You couldn't back down. We were playing a football match in Robinhood and there was this fella – Eamon – a good footballer but not as good as he thought he was. I pulled on him with the football and he said, 'Fuck you and your oul wan'. I saw red, picked up a stick and gave him a clatter with it. He went off crying to his father and the father arrived out and confronted me. I told him what his son had said and he turned around and gave the young fella a smack for insulting my mother.

I stayed in St. Cillian's in Robinhood until I was in fourth class, then myself and my mate Tony O'Keefe were sent to the Model School in Inchicore. The kids there called us culchies! They were from Ballyfermot, they'd just been moved out of the inner city, and they had totally different accents to us. The slagging we got!

Tony is dead now – everyone's dead now – but he always had a few coins in his pocket. He used to buy a ha'penny worth of honey, or a few Cleeve's Toffees. These came in big and small sizes. He shared the odd bit with me, but he made sure he kept the big ones for himself. We used to bring lunch to school – two slices of bread if I could find it; no slices of bread if I couldn't.

The master there was a man called Mr. Beatty. He wasn't a bad fella. I remember he was very impressed with myself and Tony, and told us that the day we arrived in the school was a day for Ireland. But he was fond of the drink, Mr. Beatty, and he'd often come in with a hangover. He ran a night school in his garage – charging a few bob for extra lessons in order to fund the beer. We'd try and go if we could because if you went, he'd be nicer to you during the day.

The classrooms were divided by folding doors from floor to ceiling. One day he came in a bit the worse for wear, and was having trouble opening up the partition. One of my mates – Peter – decided to help. He ran at the partition from the inside, hitting it with such force that he knocked Mr. Beatty off his feet and his glasses smashed onto the floor. Well, Mr. Beatty was beside himself with rage and took off after Peter, who dodged between the desks to avoid him. The chase went on and on around the classroom. It was hilarious and terrifying at the same time. What would he do to Peter if he caught him? But Peter escaped out the door and didn't come back till the following day, when Mr. Beatty calmed down, and saw, I think, that Peter was only trying to help.

The headmaster, Mr. Brown, lived in Knockmitten, which wasn't too far from us. He had this big case he carried with him on the back of his bike. If he had to go into town after school, he'd often get me to wheel the bike home for him. I never got anything for this service, but I thought it might keep him off my back. I'm not sure if it worked or not. There was one day, somebody wrote on the blackboard: 'You are a brat for cursing' and when nobody owned up to it, Mr. Brown decided he'd take a sample of all our writing. Foolishly, I copied out the words in the exact same style as I saw on the board. So he thought it was me that had done it, and this man, whose bike I used to take home all the time, whacked me as hard as he could six times with the cane. He put every last dram of energy into those swipes, and he was sweating after it. I had small little hands, and he left them in bits. Blistered and cut. Ma wanted to go into him after that – I was an innocent man after all – but I said no. 'It would only be worse for me Mam.'

Another time, I was on the Gaelic football team and the master kept shouting at me from the sideline. I got fed up with it, so I told him to fuck off. After the match, I was brought back before the headmaster and I got six of the best again. I suppose I couldn't complain about those ones.

I hated school. It just wasn't for me and when I left, I was glad to be gone.

Chapter 3
Toffee, Theft and Cow Guts

My brother Alan – or Ali as we called him – was a foreman in a sweet factory. He gave me my first job, and I was thrilled to get it. Money at last! Food! And I could finally do something about my clothes. I saw this suit in a shop window which cost 36 shillings – exactly what I was earning for a week's work. So I saved up and bought it. It was a beautiful grey suit and fit perfectly. I was thrilled with it.

The job itself was less than thrilling. We all sat around a big steel table, two metres square. The hot toffee was poured out and smoothed out with combs. Then, as it set, we used rollers with serrated edges to divide this great slab of toffee into small individual sweets which you'd break off and wrap in paper, then slot into the box you kept beside you. You had to work fast, like a typist in a typing pool.

We had two bosses, both ex-army men. One of them asked me to collect up the boxes and tie them up. So I did, but I'd a mate working alongside me, and he refused to give up any of the boxes he'd packed. I had no idea why.

'The boss is after telling me to take the boxes and tie them up,' I said.

But he still wouldn't give up the boxes, so there was a bit of a tussle and the box he gave me wasn't the kind you put toffee in. My brother stopped the flight, then turned to me and insisted I go tell the boss that *I* hit your man and not the other way round. He was trying to impress the other guys round the table, to show how much control he had over me. But he didn't get his way. I refused to do it and we all went back to work.

At the time, we used to rush home from work every lunchtime to listen to *The Kennedys of Castleross*, which was a radio soap opera that everyone was addicted to. One time, Alan had me on the crossbar and my mate on the carrier at the back, and this copper stopped us. I'll never forget his name: McIntyre. A red-headed bollix. He summonsed us, we were brought to court and fined five shillings each. That was a big chunk out of the 36 bob I was earning. A bob, I should say, is a shilling. While we're at it, a shilling was worth twelve old pence, and there were twenty of them in a pound. Then there were dollars and half dollars. At the time, a dollar was worth five shillings, so if you bet someone half a dollar, you bet them two bob and six pence, or two and six for short. Everyone got that?

Anyway, this McIntyre was one of the reasons I was terrified of the police. Another time, not long before I left school, I was waiting to cross the old Naas Road. This sand lorry was trundling in my direction. McIntyre was there and he kept telling me to go ahead and cross. He wanted to test your man's brakes. I wouldn't go, it was too dangerous, and the copper ate the head off me.

Years later I met his son in a pub: a big fat fella. He couldn't stop hiccupping. I said to him, 'I bet you ten bob I can stop you hiccupping.'

'Go way,' he said.

'I'm telling you. I can stop you hiccupping.'

'Alright so.'

I said to him, 'Right!' and I moved my hands over his chest like I was doing a magical spell. Then I said to him, 'Now, you hiccup!' When he didn't, I repeated the order. 'Come on! Hiccup!'

He says, 'I can't.'

'That'll be ten bob,' I said. I wouldn't have taken the money only for the way his father used to treat me. What had I done? I'd only given him a little fright; I'd learned that that was all you ever needed to do to get rid of the hiccups. Afterwards, he used to come looking for me when he had them. He was an awful man for the beer and was a martyr to hiccups.

I'd another run in with the police around this time. Not McIntyre, I couldn't blame him for this one.

I was sitting around the house one Sunday afternoon and this fella I knew – I couldn't call him a friend exactly, more of an acquaintance, knocked on the door. Francis. I won't give his full name. There was a car pulled up at the kerb. He nodded at it. 'The boss let me borrow the car from work. Do yourself and Tommy want to go for a spin?'

'Yeah.'

So I whistled for Tommy, he came over and we piled into the car. As we were motoring down the road, we met another friend of mine out walking with his girlfriend. Paddy Gleeson.

'Do ye want to go for a spin up the mountains Paddy?'

Paddy and his girlfriend climbed in and off we went again.

Now, I didn't know how to drive at the time. I was only fourteen; fifteen on the outside, but I knew that Francis was making a pig's arse of it. I was pretty sure from the sound of the engine that he was in the wrong gear almost all the time. Next thing, there was a hollow sort of grinding noise and the car rolled to a stop. Francis kept pumping the clutch, but you could see that it wasn't giving him any resistance. I didn't know what was wrong at the time, but of course now I know that he'd burned out the clutch.

He was a bit panicky. 'Lads,' he says, 'you'll have to give me a hand to get the car back.'

So we abandoned ship, walked back down until we got a bus stop, then took a bus to the garage where Francis worked. Paddy and his girlfriend took their leave of us at this point, so it was just me, Francis and Tommy. By now, I was pretty sure that no one had given Francis permission to take any car out of the garage, but here we were 'borrowing' another car to go back up the mountains to try to get the first one home.

We got up there anyway without burning out any more clutches. Francis took out the rope he brought and tied one end to the good car and the other to the front axle of the banjaxed car and off we went, Francis in front, me steering the car behind him.

We were halfway down the mountain when the cops appeared in the rear-view mirror, blue lights flashing. I felt my hands go weak on the steering wheel. I barely had the strength to steer the car into the side of the road.

When the big country cop told me to get out of the car, I stammered out the truth. Francis borrowed the car, the car broke down, so we borrowed another to tow it back. He didn't believe a word of it. Myself, Tommy and Francis were bundled into the cop car, driven down to Rathfarnham and put in the cells. The cells! I was horrified. My dad was four or five years dead at this stage, but I kept thinking, what would have thought? What would he have said?

I was sitting inside in the cell, shitting myself when this detective came in. You could tell by the way he held himself that he was a senior man – he wasn't in uniform, and he had a quiet sort of a confidence about him. He was friendly too.

'You look like a right gurrier,' he said, but there was a bit of a twinkle in his eye. 'What happened?'

I told him the truth again. Nobody stole anything. Francis worked in the garage and borrowed the two cars. Francis told us that the boss said it was ok.

'We weren't stealing it, we were just going for a jaunt in it.'

Meanwhile, in the other cell, Francis was hanging me. He told the coppers that it was all my idea, that I'd made him take the car, that I'd burned out the clutch, that I'd made him commandeer a second car to rescue the first.

My mother found the fiver needed to bail us out and Ali came out to Rathfarnham with it. He gave me some clatter as soon as we were clear of the barracks.

I'm not sure I slept at all in the weeks coming up to the court case, I was so nervous.

But that wasn't the worst of it. Francis' family had a bit of a reputation for violence. That's part of the reason why I didn't normally pal around with him. But there was a banging at the door one evening and it was Francis's brother. He had a slash-hook. Gerry went out to him. He was always my protector, Gerry. He's the one kept me in line, and made sure too that no one messed with me.

Your man says, 'If that young fella doesn't admit to taking the cars, he's fucked.'

Gerry just laughed at him. 'Take that fuckin' thing out of here, you ugly bollix.'

When the time came anyway, myself and Tommy met on the steps of the court, both of us in suits, both of us pale as plucked chickens. The same detective I'd met in the cells in Rathfarnham came out and gave each of us a cigarette before lighting up a butt for himself.

'Don't worry lads,' he said, 'ye just tell the truth.'

A little while later, when the judge asked me what happened, that's what I did. I told the truth. So did Tommy. But Francis stuck to his guns and made out that it was all my idea. The judge didn't believe him. The case against us was dismissed, but Francis got six months.

At the time, Big Tony was working in a butcher's shop in Clondalkin (this was before he did the bank job). He wanted to pack it in, so he asked me if I wanted the job instead. I was fed up with the sweet shop, fed up with Alan throwing his weight around, so I said, yeah, I'd do it.

The funny thing was, when Tony worked in the butcher's, the boss used to give him all the takings from the week to bring down to the bank in Clondalkin, and despite the fact that he had all this money every week, he never took a bob, he never did anything wrong. I suppose gangsters don't dip their hand into the takings. They shoot up banks with guns.

Anyway, this job mostly involved delivering meat, but that wasn't all of it. They had their own slaughter house, and it was my job to clean out the guts of the animals that had been killed. I had to shove a hose into these intestines and flush all the shite out of them. These would then be boiled up and fed to the pigs. An awful job. Terrible. The smell would get into your hair and your clothes and no amount of washing would get it out.

The boss was only a young fella himself, but he was a big strapping lad. My first job in the morning was to get him out of bed. I'd have to throw pebbles up at his bedroom window without breaking it. You couldn't knock on the door because he slept in an extension at the back of the house and wouldn't have been able to hear you.

He used to give me ten bob extra for going round collecting bills on a Monday afternoon. This was much nicer work than cleaning out fresh guts, but it wasn't easy. There was one fella, Paddy Crosbie. He used to be on the radio, he hosted a famous programme called 'The School around the Corner', where he'd interview schoolchildren and get funny stories out of them and that. To listen to him, you'd think he was a lovely fella, but he didn't treat me very well. He lived in one of the new houses in Clondalkin and to be honest, I was afraid of my life of him. He wouldn't let me in the gate. If I knocked on the door, he'd roar at me to get back outside onto the footpath, no matter what the weather was doing.

He wasn't there one day so I collected the money from his wife instead. But I was jumpy in case he showed up, so I rushed the job a bit. When I got back, the boss took all the money I'd collected and counted it. It was short ten bob. I said, 'I think that was Mrs. Crosbie, I'm nearly sure it was.'

Why? Because I had counted out the money everywhere else. But when the boss called her up, she said that she'd paid the full score. 'He counted out the money in front of me.'

I couldn't blame her for that, I was nervous and had just gone through the motions of counting.

When he came off the phone to her, he said, 'I'll have to let you go after the weekend.'

I shrugged. 'Alright.'

I worked out the week and as I was leaving on the Friday, he says to me, 'I'll see you Monday.'

'You sacked me the other day,' I said, 'and accused me of stealing.'

'Ah forget about it,' he says.

'No,' I said, 'I wouldn't work for you. You don't trust me.'

So I went home and told my mother. She says, 'Go work for someone better than yourself.'

I was only fourteen at this stage, but I had a sense of my own value. I said, 'There's nobody better than me, Ma. We're all the same.'

I got a job quickly enough after that – in a garage. Back then, there was a big garage and a cafe on the corner of the Naas Road and the Long Mile Road.

This was this oul fella used to come in; he had a couple of big sand lorries. Back then, the petrol pumps stood all around the building. This guy used to pull up to pump Number 6, say, then tell me to almost fill the tank but knock it off when it was ten or fifteen gallons from full. Then he'd tell me to start it up again and fill it the rest of the way, so that it looked as if I'd only done it once. I'd call out, 'Pump number six, ten gallons.' He might have forty or fifty gallons in it, and he never got found out. I never said anything to anyone about it, because I sort of admired his brass neck, and I suppose I was probably a bit of an aspiring chancer myself.

Another time, a man arrived in with a van packed to the roof with sweets. He had a puncture, but couldn't find a place to put the jack. I was still small so I got under the van to see if I could help. As soon as I crawled out from under it again, the whole thing collapsed under the weight of the sweets. If I'd still been there, I'd have been a goner.

I didn't like this job much, so I didn't stay in it too long. One of my mates worked in a company that made lockers and office furniture and got me in there. It wasn't a bad job on the face of it, but the problem was the spray paint they used on finished products. The air would be thick with it – you could hardly breathe. I got two pound, ten shillings a week to breathe in all these fumes. It was nearly worse than cleaning out guts.

I was at work one day, making this office furniture and breathing in these fumes when one of my pals from the Long Mile Road – Denis – came in to see me.

'I'm after being sacked,' he said, 'so I'm going away, I'm going to Blackpool on Friday. Will you come?'

'Wait there,' I said.

I stopped what I was doing and went and knocked on the boss's door. 'Mr. Brown,' I said, 'would there be any chance of a raise?'

He said, 'Would you like to leave?'

I said, 'Yeah, I'll leave Friday.'

In the end there were three of us. Myself, Denis and another friend of his – Christy. I said nothing about leaving Dublin to my mother, because she wouldn't have let me go. I slipped off without saying a word.

Chapter 4
Hunger-by-the-Sea

I was after buying a gabardine topcoat off a fella in Walkinstown. Cost me £2. I got it dyed black. I also robbed two of my brother's shirts – cheap oul Nylon things. There were no toothbrushes or toothpaste at the time, so all I had when I left home that morning were those two cheap shirts and the coat. But when I got into town, I decided I didn't need the coat. It was still early in the spring, it wasn't warm, but neither of the other two had coats. So I left it in a toilet. I felt like a criminal doing it, and it wasn't long after that – and for a long time afterwards – I thought about that coat and missed it badly. I was a stupid kid.

It was my first time on a boat, if you don't count the barges on the canal. We were freezing and throwing up the whole way across. We stopped first in Birkenhead to let the cattle off, then it was on to Liverpool.

As soon as we landed, we got a taxi down to Blackpool. I couldn't get over how cheap this taxi was. Everything was cheaper in England at that time.

Not cheap enough, it would turn out.

We found a dosshouse in Blackpool – what would be called a homeless shelter today. It was full of tramps and hoboes, but it was grand and warm, with a big furnace going constantly. You could buy a penny's worth of butter, tuppence worth of bread, and they'd give you a long fork to toast the bread in front of the furnace. That's how we survived, eating bread and butter – or chips if we could afford them, but of course the money wasn't long running out, and at that point, it was bread and butter or nothing. We slept in a big dorm full of bunk-beds and made friends with a fella from Meath – Phil – who was also staying there, and a number of men who were Scots-Irish.

There was a funny mix in that dosshouse. Some fellas had posh accents. These were dropouts, who gave up whatever they had and took to the roads. They used to have these big intellectual arguments in front of the furnace at night. I used to be fascinated listening to them talking about politics and art and culture and all that sort of stuff.

One night anyway, some fella tried to get into bed beside Phil, and that led to a big fight and a hullaballoo and that was the end of the dosshouse. We were all thrown out.

Things got a lot harder from then on. We used to sleep in tram shelters, but the coppers would come along and move us on. 'You can't sleep here. This is a holiday resort.'

So we would walk out of town into the sand-dunes, and try to sleep there. I used to gather up newspapers and stuff them inside my clothes to try to build up a bit of heat. I'd only ever manage to sleep for an hour, and then it was up and off again. We spent the nights just walking the town. Summer or not, the hours of darkness were freezing. When the sun shone, it was grand, but if there was a wind off the sea – and there often was – it would blow sand and spray everywhere. The backs of the hotels which lined the waterfront would often be an inch deep in sand blown in. I often thought with regret of that fine coat I'd abandoned in the toilet in Dublin and wonder who was wearing it now.

No matter how bad it got, we never stole and we never begged – well, almost.

Christy gave up and joined the army. Phil left to go somewhere else – I don't remember where, so it was just me and Denis, who was a year younger than me. Every single morning, we'd go from one hotel to the next, looking for work as kitchen porters.

They'd all say, 'Come back again Paddy, come back again.' After a while these chefs would get to know us by name. 'Not today Rory, but come back again.' Sometimes we'd ask for a sandwich, and often we got it.

The rest of the time went in looking for food or shelter. We used to sneak into the church when no one was looking, get over near the heater and let on to be praying, just to get warm for a bit.

I found out that the there were a couple of Irish priests living next to the church, so I said to Denis: 'Come on we'll go up to the priests' house and ask them for something to eat, maybe get a cup of tea.'

So we rang the doorbell and one of the priests came out, all in black and a bitter look about him. 'What can I do for you?'

'Father we haven't eaten for three days, would you give us a bit of bread and a cup of tea?'

'Go home.'

'Father we haven't got the money to go home.'

He slammed the door in our faces. Down in the church at mass, the same man would be going on about the need to donate money to those less fortunate than ourselves. Right at that moment, I felt as though there was no one less fortunate than myself and Denis.

I found out in Blackpool that it's the people who have nothing at all that tend to be the kindest. Sometimes we'd bump into the Scots Irish out of the dosshouse and they'd get us a sandwich or a bag of chips. Sometimes they might even give us a couple of bob.

We had nothing to do only walk the streets. Too hungry to be bored.

One of those Scots Irish fellas said 'Why don't you sell papers Rory?'

'How do you do that?'

'Go down to *The Evening Gazette* office and they'll give you ten papers for nothing and tell you where to stand. If you sell them, you can buy more.'

So I tried it. I got the papers, went to my spot and I did my best to sell a few. You had to call out the winners of the races as you were standing there, just to try and drum up a bit of business.

There I was anyway, shouting out, 'Two thirty winner! Two thirty winner!'

This fella runs up to me, 'Give me one of them quick Paddy!'

'What's your hurry?'

'It's only one o'clock!'

I got on alright at the job, but you'd make very little – enough to eat maybe, but not enough to get out of the weather.

I heard then there was a job going in the Ferney Hotel. One of the Irish was after leaving and they needed someone to replace him. We tossed for it – myself and Denis – and I won, so I went in the backdoor and met the woman in charge. But I had this big mop of curls at that time and I knew that she was a little bit reluctant about giving me the job. Next thing someone comes into her and says 'There's someone to see you at the front door.'

She went out and was gone for a while, and I just knew. I said to myself, 'That's Dennis.'

Eventually, she came back and said, 'Sorry, I have another man here who's more suited to the position.'

'Is his name Denis?'

'It is.'

I didn't argue. 'That's alright, thanks. Could I have a sandwich instead?'

'You can of course.'

She got me the sandwich and let me sit there to eat it.

I didn't see Denis for a while after that. Even though he'd swiped the job out from under me, I was delighted for him in a way, because he was a little bit younger than me, and he needed a job every bit as much as I did.

I continued in the same rhythm, going from hotel to hotel to hotel, meeting the same response every time. 'Come back again Rory.' I got a bit down about it to be honest, a bit depressed. Once, I saw a couple of fellas I knew from Dublin. They must have been over on holidays. Blackpool was a very popular spot back then, but I ducked into a shop so they wouldn't see me. I didn't want them to know I was skint. And I didn't want my mother finding me either. Probably the lowest point was the night I climbed the railings into a park, pulled up a load of grass and found an outdoor tap to wash it in. I tried to eat it, but it was just too hard to chew, let alone digest. No wonder horses and cows have such big teeth.

Eventually the morning came when I went to the Dorchester with the usual request and this time, the manager, Mr. Yoxall, said to me, 'Can you start at seven in the morning Rory?'

'I can!'

I don't think I was ever as relieved in my life. I didn't have a watch of course, but there was a hotel – The Cliffs – that had a big clock over the door, so that night, I never strayed too far from it. I was afraid to drop off even for an hour, in case I slept through and missed the start time. At ten to seven, I was at the backdoor of the Dorchester, where I met a waiter. We chatted, and I let it slip that I didn't have anywhere to stay. Then Mr. Yoxall came in and brought me into a back kitchen stacked with dirty dishes, cutlery and cups.

'I'll need you to wash all these,' he said, 'but first, come on in here. Your breakfast is ready.'

I followed him to the kitchen and there was a big bowl of porridge, a full English breakfast and all the toast you could eat. I couldn't believe my eyes. I was in heaven. I sat down and started shovelling food into me.

Next thing I hear, 'Wake up, Rory! Wake up!'

I was so tired, I'd fallen asleep in the middle of the food. Oh Jesus, I thought, I'm going to be sacked now.

Mr. Yoxall stood at my shoulder. 'Finish your breakfast. Don't rush it, take your time, then go in and start your work.'

I did exactly as he said. I ate until I could eat no more then I went to work, washing up all the dirty plates and cutlery and so on. A couple of hours later, Mr. Yoxall came back in and inspected the work. 'Now,' he said, 'you come along with me.'

I followed him upstairs through the hotel until we got to a bathroom on the top floor. What's he bringing me in here for? I wondered. Well, wasn't he after turning this old bathroom into a bedroom. He'd laid a row of boards down on top of the bath and put a mattress on them to make a bed.

'Make the best of that you can,' he said.

I was over the moon. I hadn't slept in anything vaguely resembling a bed in weeks.

Mrs. Yoxall was the chef at the hotel. She was a little butty woman, but lovely, as lovely as he was. Then there was Mr. Yoxall's sister, Mrs. Lightfoot, who was married to a butcher in Crewe, but worked at the hotel all week, then the husband came up to her at the weekend. Neither of these couples had children, and I think it's fair to say that over the next few months, they began to treat me like a son. It was like having four parents. They were very good to me and we got on great.

While I was there, Denis went back home to visit his mother, who told my mother where I was. So one morning, Mr. Yoxall comes in with a letter addressed to Master Rowland McClelland.

'Is this you Rory?'

'It is.'

'Is your name Rory or Rowland?'

'It's Rowland,' I said, 'but that was always a bit posh for me, so I changed it to Rory.'

Ma gave out like hell – why wouldn't she? She wanted to know why I ran away and all that. I wrote back to her and enclosed a few bob.

Meanwhile, I was getting on great at the Dorchester. They'd hired me as a kitchen porter, but I ended up doing everything. To this day, I can cook anything thanks to the Yoxhalls. Mr. Yoxall's wife and sister were just the loveliest women. The sister was quite elderly, but very sprightly. She used to wash and iron my clothes. There was this Scottish fella working there too. He could neither read nor write, so I used to write letters home to his girlfriend for him. One time, the two of us went out and got very drunk. I was sick as a pig the next day, but Mrs. Lightfoot minded me. She sent me round to the shops to get some sort of brandy which I was supposed to drink as a cure. I suffered through the day, but I was right as rain the next morning. They used to make me go to mass too, and they were Protestants! I went – like an eejit. There'd often be ferocious winds blowing in off the sea. I remember one Sunday morning I had to dash from lamppost to lamppost just to keep from being blown away. I was still a scrawny, light little fella. I was lucky I didn't blow out to sea.

Throughout the summer season, there were big shows in all the theatres every night.

Comedy mostly, but also singing and dancing. We had sixteen chorus girls staying at the Dorchester that first year. These girls were appearing in a show on the North Pier with Tommy Cooper, who was a big star at the time. They were chaperoned at all times by a woman called Miss Finnegan. She was about forty, and she was beautiful, but by Jaysus, everyone was afraid of her: me, the girls, even Mrs. Yoxhall. She made sure everyone of her performers was back at the hotel right after the show and didn't stir out afterwards.

  They used tease me the whole time. Trying to get a rise out of me. It didn't take much! I had a right bit of fun with those girls, and they gave me tickets to all the shows, which were amazing. I saw Tommy Cooper, Bradley Walsh, Charlie Drake, Bob Monkhouse. They gave me tickets for some of the funny little sideshows that used to be on. I remember seeing 'The Ugliest Woman in the World!' – it was just a man who needed a bit of a wash. I used to go to the pictures too; I loved cowboy films in particular. After I got the job, I didn't mix much with people outside the hotel. The Yoxalls became like family.

I planned to head home in July, but Mr. Yoxall took me aside and asked me to stay until the end of September.

'My wife likes working with you,' he said, 'she gets a bit anxious, but she's comfortable with you.'

He told me that if I waited, he'd pay my airfare home. An airplane! I'd never even seen one up close. Well, that was too good an offer to resist.

There were these two sisters working in the hotel. Scottish girls. I fancied the two of them, but the younger one – Eileen – in particular. She was only fifteen – the same age I was. We didn't really get up to anything. I remember the boss came into my room one time and we were both lying on top of my bed, but we were fully clothed and were just talking, so he didn't give out.

Anyway, September came and went and eventually it was time for my flight home. As I was walking across the car park from the taxi rank to the terminal building, I heard my name being called, and when I turned around, who was it only Eileen. She was after getting Mrs. Lightfoot to drive her to the airport to beg me to stay. She was bawling crying. It was like something out of a film. I was so touched, I nearly started crying myself, but I wanted to go home, and I was mad excited to be in an airplane, so that was the end of that little romance.

The airplane journey was amazing, but when I got home, Ma brought me down to earth with a bang. She gave out hell to me for going off without a word. I gave her twenty quid to soften the blow – that was a lot of money in those days. I stayed at home until the money ran out, then I went back to Blackpool and slotted into my old place with the Yoxalls. Eileen had gone back to Scotland at that stage. I remember we had Ruby Murray staying with us this time. She was a huge singing star, with a lovely soft voice.

But I'd seen all that Blackpool had to show me, and I started to get itchy feet. I thought it was time I went south to London.

Chapter 5
A short Chapter about Teddy Boys

By the time I landed a job at Express Dairies in Highbury later that year, I was just sixteen years old. I was living like a man, but I was still only a boy.

Getting a place to stay turned out to be a bit of an ordeal. I had two friends living in a flat in a place called Aubert Park which was also in Highbury, but it took me ages to find it. Like most people, I used to ask coppers for directions. None of them had heard of Aubert Park. I don't know how many I asked before one of them said, 'Oh! You mean Oh-bert park.'

I was just pronouncing it wrong, or else no one could understand my Dublin accent. I found the place where my two mates, John and Christy were living, but there was no room at the inn. They directed me instead to this house a couple of streets away where a little old woman was offering digs. She welcomed me in and the price was alright, but the next morning, she gave me my breakfast on a dirty plate. And when I looked around in the cold light of day, I could see that the place was filthy. So I just paid her the score and went back to the two boys in Aubert or Oh-bert Park. Together, we managed to find another bed and slot it into the room and that was alright. I was set up.

Arsenal are at home in Highbury of course. I'll never forget the first match I ever went to. It was overwhelming. There were no seats at the time, it was all terraces. I remember walking into the ground and being confronted by a sea of red faces. The biggest crowd I'd ever seen before that was at mass. To be honest, the number of people frightened me.

We used to go to a club called the Hollywood Club in Finsbury Park. The stage was nearly ten feet off the ground, so if there was any trouble, the band would be safe.

Remember Big Tony's ma thought I was a Teddy Boy? Well, in London, I became a Teddy Boy. All my friends were Teddy Boys. We had the sideburns – or sideboards as the Londoners called them – the Elvis hair, coat down to your knees and a pair of crepe-soled shoes. You'd wear a bootlace instead of a tie. In the dance halls, we'd be on one side, the cockneys would be on the other and the foreigners – the Greeks and so on – would be down near the stage.

Sometimes one crowd would pick a fight with us or we'd pick a fight with one of them. Usually though, it wouldn't turn into a mass brawl. The big fellas would step in and take care of any agro before it kicked off.

The club was owned by an Irishman – he was from down the country and had a big thick culchie accent. One night, we were all outside waiting for him to let us in and this fella walks up to the hatch. He was obviously a culchie too, but well dressed. He slapped a ten bob note down, but the boss was standing nearby and he took the note and handed it back to him.

'Sorry,' he said, 'members only.'

After your man went away, he said to us, 'He looked like a troublemaker lads. Ye go on in, ye're alright.'

He knew us, he knew we weren't any trouble. At least not that much. Better the devil you know I suppose.

It was in London too that I fell in love for the first time. Jill was her name. Gorgeous. Beautiful brown eyes and jet black hair. She was 21, I was still only 16. We had a great time together. I was head over heels in love. She worked in Express Dairies too. When no one was looking, I'd grab her, pull her into a little nook in the wall and kiss her.

The job itself wasn't exactly exciting. Wheeling around trolleys, mixing great big vats of Christmas pudding and cakes and things. It could be heavy work at times, but I was young and fit. It didn't take anything out of me.

There was another girl in the job that fancied me – at least I thought she did. She used to warn me off Jill. 'She's on the game, you know that, don't you?' I didn't believe her. I thought she was just jealous.

Christmas was coming and Jill was heading home to Cheltenham where her family lived.

'Will you come with me?' she said.

'Where would I stay?'

'You'll stay with me in my room.'

I said no. I didn't have the nerve to go into her parents' house and sleep in the same room with her and us unmarried. I just couldn't do it.

So I stayed in London that Christmas. And to be honest about it, I wasn't faithful to her. I was after discovering women and I just couldn't get enough. Jill came back down in

January. I remember I was so excited before she arrived, but then she told me that she'd slept with two other fellas while she was away. Two! That was that. It was over. She broke my heart. It took me years and years to get over Jill.

I got caught too though. At that time, you carried a photograph of yourself, to give to your girl or your fella. The one I went out with while Jill was away showed my photograph to someone who half knew Jill, and your one says, 'That's Jill's boyfriend!' So that gig was up too.

Afterwards, I was on a bus into Russell Square and I met a friend of Jill's – Wendy. She told me that she was on her way into town to meet a Sheik.

'Why?' I said.

'You know,' she winked.

'Is he giving you a job or something?'

'Or something.'

It was only then it began to dawn on me what that girl had said at work might be true.

'Does Jill do that too? *Meet* people.'

Wendy nodded.

You live and learn.

I ended up getting sacked out of that job. It was a strange thing. I was working with a couple of Dubliners and a number of Greeks. The Greeks began to accuse me of stabbing a mate of theirs in Marble Arch. I didn't know where Marble Arch was, and besides, I never left Highbury, and besides, I never stabbed anyone. A bit of a row broke out on the job over it and I got sacked. The foreman liked me however and said that though he had to let me go, he would give me a job working nights. I said alright. It might have been Greeks and Dubliners by day, but those nightshifts were mostly run by South Americans. I was there a couple of weeks when one of them comes up to me and says, 'My friend would like to fight you.'

'What?'

'My friend would like to fight you.'

I said, 'Tell him I'll fight him for a pound.'

'You no understand,' he said, 'he wants ...'

Turns out he didn't want a fight, he wanted something else entirely. So then a real fight broke out over this and I ended up throwing a fella into a big tub of water, and that was the end of that. I got sacked again.

John, one of the lads I was staying with, was at a loose end too. He made a new suggestion. 'Will we join the army?'

Chapter 6
Triggers

It was that simple. We decided we were going to do it, so we just did it. We took a bus down to the recruitment office in Kentish Town and signed up. They gave us rail tickets for Winchester, and when we got there, we were directed to an army barracks where we were given uniforms and assigned bunks in a big dormitory. There were a pile of lads there before us, a few bullies among them. That first night, after we went to bed, they started in on us.

'Paddy! Lie to attention!'

I got out of bed, 'Fuck off!' I said, 'Don't try that with me!'

By then I'd learned that you had to appear tough, even if you weren't. You had to give the impression that you were ready for anything, even if you weren't. Otherwise they'd eat you alive.

The following day, I was passing through the billet and someone started passing remarks about Ireland.

I rounded on him. 'Do you want your fuckin' nose broke?'

'Alright, Paddy, I didn't mean any harm.'

'Don't fuckin' call me Paddy for starters, and don't try belittle me or you'll take the consequences.'

It was all front. You had to be able to put up a front like that, you just had to. Maybe though, if you do it often enough, that bit of hardness seeps into you.

The training was very tough. We'd go out marching in full battle dress, rifle and all. *Left wheel!* and you'd turn left without breaking stride. *Left turn!* Stop, turn and off you go again. The whole idea behind all of this drilling is that the orders go so deep that you'll always do immediately what you're told, you won't question anything. We had to do these twenty mile route marches, carrying your full gear on your back. The bags weren't huge but by God they were heavy. I carried a rifle; that was my rank: rifleman. The fella marching on my left was a big fat Londoner. He was a machine gunner, but on these long marches, he couldn't manage the weight of the machine gun so I'd swap with him just so he could make it through.

Here's the strange thing. The minute I took the Lee Enfield rifle into my hands, it felt good. It felt *right*. I took to shooting practise like a duck to water and got very good at it very quickly. I'd never been a great footballer or a great boxer or anything, but now all of a sudden, I found my niche. How did this happen? I have no idea, but I suppose it must have been a natural gift from my father.

Even now, I can feel the weight of the rifle in my arms. You take it up to your shoulder and place the butt firmly against it. There's going to be recoil, but if you have the butt square and tight against your shoulder so that there's no play in it, there's no room for the rifle to jerk backwards. You line the tip of the barrel up and there's a treaded nut to adjust the sight. You don't pull the trigger, you don't jerk it. The sergeant used to say, 'Take the first pressure ... and squeeze.' You always keep your head in position until after the bullet is gone.

Later in the year, when we were halfway through basic training, they held a shooting competition among all six hundred recruits, and I won it.

Our Sergeant – Sainsbury was his name – liked me, and sort of took me under his wing. He didn't care where I was from, he only cared about how good a solider I could be. When I won that competition, he took me out to the parade ground to prepare me for the presentation ceremony. I was glad to have that little rehearsal because I was quite a shy person and wasn't fond of the attention.

For the ceremony itself, the entire training regiment were lined up in the parade ground. Rows and rows of men standing in tight formation while the CO – Handscombe was his name – addressed us. I remember his voice booming out over the PA. My name was called, I had to step back, turn around and march down this long line of soldiers to the bandstand where I was told to stand at ease. Myself and Handscombe had a bit of a chat. He asked me where I was from, and I told him about my da serving in the First World War. He gave me my medal and back I went to my place.

Of course, you had to be immaculately turned out all the time – which suited me. The boots that they issued you with had blisters all over the leather. You had to get a hot spoon, put some black polish on it, then keep running it to and fro over the blisters. If you did it right, the boots would shine as if they were patent leather.

Because I was such a great shot, they kept entering me in army shooting competitions. I went all over the UK and won piles of medals. One time, I was in a place called Aldershot, where the paratroopers are based. Those fellas don't sleep on beds, they have mattresses on the floor. That's how we slept when we were there. That evening, we were all in the Naffi – which is what they call the bar. They have them in every barracks. This paratrooper started picking on me. He was looking for a fight, and I was a bit nervous because we were on his turf, but I'd made a few mates in my company by that stage and they were all around me. They were cockneys, and they told him to fuck off. Then some of his mates showed up and took him away. Afterwards, one of them told us that he was only picking on me because a war was brewing in Cypress and your man was trying to get into trouble so that he wouldn't have to go.

Sergeant Sainsbury's attitude seemed to change after I began racking up all these shooting awards. He started giving me a really hard time. 'McClelland, that's not good enough.' I knew that I was better at drilling and keeping myself neat and tidy than anyone else in the company, so I couldn't understand why he was always singling me out. I pulled him up one day. You're not supposed to do that, but I did.

'Sergeant,' I said, 'Can I have a word with you?'

'Yes McClelland.'

I said, 'You seem to pick on me for absolutely everything, but I'm better than all the others at most of this stuff.'

'Yes, McClelland, you are and you've got to be, because I have you marked for promotion. If you're going to be promoted, you have to be the best solider in this company.'

That gave me something to think about.

If you were going to be a sniper – and I had the right skills for it – you needed to be very fit, because you once you took your shot, you had to be able to get away from wherever you were very bloody quick. So I spent in a lot of time in the gym. I was there one day, going up and down the climbing rope. There was this other fella there too, a fella by the name of Danny Chippendale. He was a boxer, and before the army, he had been on the point of turning professional. While I was going up and down the rope, he was in the ring sparring with himself. I finished up anyway and went over to him.

'Danny,' I said, 'I don't know how to box, will you show us a few moves?'

He said he would, but he didn't show me anything useful, he just kept hitting me.

'Enough!' I said. 'I asked you to show me something, not use me for a punch bag.'

Now, when the mail came in, it was just like you'd see in the films. Everyone would flood over to where the sergeant was handing it out. Jill wrote to me the whole time I was in the army; long letters written on scented paper, telling me how much she loved me. I still loved her, I missed her like crazy, and to get a letter from her was a real treat. So this one time anyway, the sergeant called my name and I could tell by the envelope that it was from her. I was thrilled. Then I looked up and Danny was standing there, scowling at me. 'What the fuck are you so happy about?' he says.

I told him to fuck off and he came at me.

Now, if I have to fight someone, I will, no problem. Danny might have been a great boxer, but boxers are no good outside the ring. They wouldn't stand a chance with a wrestler. And I might have been scrawny, but I was strong from all the rope climbing, so I managed to get him on the ground. I was on top of him, hitting him, half afraid to let him go to be totally honest. This corporal dragged me off eventually, and Danny got to his feet and drew back, his hands up. He didn't give me any more trouble.

It wasn't long after that, I was out on the rifle range one day and things nearly went very badly wrong. Instead of the usual Lee Enfield, we were firing Sten guns, which are a sort of light machine gun. Everybody got their own target, which was a picture of a German. It would flap up and you'd have to hit it quick as you could. I was down on the ground shooting away, when the Sergeant – not Sainsbury, another fella – who was walking up and down the line, says to me, 'Reload!'

These magazines held thirty-two bullets, and it was hard to know, when you were firing, if you had any left or not, but I thought that I did.

'There's still a couple in the spout, Sir,' I said, which meant that though the magazine might be empty, there were still two rounds in the barrel itself.

The sergeant scowled at me. 'Reload McClelland!'

At this point, a corporal had gone up to the target to check my score. As part of the process of reloading the gun, you had to pull the trigger, and when I did, three bullets shot out. By some miracle, I was pointing the gun at the ground so that's where the bullets went, but that corporal had no idea how close he came to getting shot in the back. If that had happened, I'd have been fucked, but so too would that sergeant. I don't know what told me that there were bullets left in the barrel, because you couldn't count them as you shot; they came out too fast.

As well as shooting, they taught you how to use grenades. These are the Mills Grenades, like you'd see in the films. They look like pineapples. We were given two each. When it was my turn, I picked up the first, pulled the ring, threw it out of the trench then ducked down to protect myself against the explosion. That turned out to be a mistake. Sergeant Sainsbury turned and hit me a box that made my head ring. After the grenade exploded, he roared at me, 'The enemy could have thrown that grenade back at you! You could have been killed.'

He explained that these grenades had a nine second fuse, so you had to stay alert and on the watch to make sure no one tried to send the thing back to you. When I was getting ready to throw the second grenade, he said to me 'Don't move until I do.'

So I threw it, and waited … and waited … and waited. The only thing stopping me ducking down was the knowledge that if I messed it up a second time, he wouldn't punch me, he'd hit me with the butt of the rifle. After what seemed like an eternity, he roared, 'Down!'

We had barely made it into the trench before it went off. You could feel the wind of it.

'Jesus,' said Sainsbury, 'I nearly killed us both.'

Reveille was at 6:30 in the morning, then you'd go on parade at seven, and after that, you got your breakfast. One morning anyway, we were all standing to attention on parade and the sergeant was walking up and down between the rows of soldiers. Next thing, I hear him roar, 'Soldier! Your neck is dirty.'

I knew without even having to turn around that he was talking about to my mate John. He wasn't dirty, he just had really dark skin on his neck. I knew this because I'd said it to him one time. 'Jaysus John, would you not wash your neck, it's filthy.'

But he showed me that it wasn't dirty at all, it just looked dirty.

The sergeant roars, 'Everybody confined to barracks tonight.'

Shite, I said to myself. I knew there'd be trouble after that. I'd made a few friends among the cockneys we shared the billet with, but getting confined to barracks would test those friendships.

So we all had to turn in at seven o'clock that night. Myself and John had bunks in the corner: me on top, him on the bottom. Right from the moment the door closed, I knew we were in trouble. There was a real edge to the atmosphere. Everyone was muttering to everyone else. I heard someone say, 'fuckin' Irish'. People were giving us awful dirty looks. Next thing they all started gathering in the centre of the room, all thirty of them, pulling their beds closer and whispering and working out what they'd do with us.

John was a year older than me, but he was terrified. I could see his body shaking under the blankets.

I said to myself, 'What am I going to do? I have to do something. What would my da do?'

As the ringleaders stood up and started towards us, I said, 'Fuck it,' and took my rifle from the rack. I grabbed my bayonet and fixed it. They give you three blank bullets, just for show. They're yours to keep. They won't kill you, but they'll blind you. So I put one bullet up the spout and two in the magazine. I was very fit by this time. All the marching and the rope climbing had me ready for anything. I used to be able to hold a bicycle pump in both hands and jump through it.

What happened next felt like it was happening in slow motion. They were coming closer and closer. Someone said, 'We're getting kept in because of that dirty Paddy.'

So I jumped out in front of our two bunks. 'Come on you bastards, I'll blow the fuckin' bollix off yiz.'

The three fellas in front of the mob froze, but they didn't go back. I drew the rifle up to my shoulder slowly and took aim. Everyone knew I was the best shot there, not that you'd need to be much of a marksman if the target was only a few feet away. But they saw my fingers flex around the barrel of the gun.

'I'll blind the next man takes a step in my direction.'

Hands started to go up.

'Calm down now Paddy.'

'Me name's not fuckin' Paddy.'

'Alright Rory, no harm done. We're all pals here.'

I took a step forward. 'Then fuck off back to your own bunks.'

I was like a mad man. The eyes nearly out of my head. I was ready to go for them. But they backed off. I stood there, knuckles white on the gun until they settled the beds back into place and went off to sleep themselves. Never a word was spoken about it again.

Not long after this, my mate John got leave and went back to Ireland. That was that – he never came back. But I had a knack for the army.

They used to bring us out on what they called field craft exercises. You're given these goggles that reduce your visibility to almost nothing, then you have to make your way on your belly across open ground to where the enemy is hiding. While I was doing this, I overheard two officers who were observing manoeuvres talking about me.

'Who's that?'

'McClelland, sir. He's Irish.'

'He's damn good at this, isn't he?'

I had no idea at the time, but my army days were coming to an end.

There's a place called Bisley in Surrey, and every year there's a big shooting competition which brings in competitors from all over the British Commonwealth. That year, our regiment – the Rifle Brigade – were co-hosting the competition with the King's Royal

Rifle Core. Myself and my mate Terry were working in the kitchen, washing pots and pans and peeling potatoes. Miserable work. You'd have a big pile of potatoes and there might be half a dozen of you sitting around it, peeling and peeling and peeling. Myself and Terry were just after putting in a five hour shift and were on our lunch break. As we were walking to the mess tent, this RSM – a regimental sergeant major – stopped us and pointed at Terry's shoes.

'You're wearing civilian shoes, solider.'
'Yes sir, sorry sir.'
'Watch company orders tonight. You'll be on report.'

Company orders were posted on a notice board every evening. If your name appeared there, that meant you'd be up in front of a disciplinary hearing the following day.

Next thing the bastard turned to me and asked me my name. I told him.

'McClelland, your buttons are dirty.'

I wasn't having this. 'Sir, I've been working in the kitchen for five hours, what do you expect?'

I don't know what pissed him off more, the buttons or me giving him backchat, but my name was up beside Terry's that evening, and the following day we had to appear in front of the CO, who was flanked on either side by two captains. The RSM who was the cause of it all was there too. The charges were read out and the CO barked: 'Seven days confined to barracks.'

I wasn't having this. 'I was working in a kitchen for five hours!'

'Dismissed!'

This is where all the drilling was supposed to kick in. We'd spent hundreds of hours being told what to do – *Attention! About face! Left wheel! Right turn!* So when you heard these orders, you were supposed to carry them out without thinking. And I did, I came to attention, saluted, turned about and marched out. But I was not happy.

Afterwards, I was back in my tent and the RSM came looking for me. 'You could have been done for dumb insubordination!' he said, 'but I'll help you.'

'I don't want your help,' I said, 'you've helped me enough. I thought this was a man's army. I thought I'd be treated like a man, not like a fool.'

He wasn't too pleased by that. 'What are you going to do?' he asked me.

'Time will tell.'

I knew exactly what I was going to do. I went and collected my credits – meaning my savings. Terry did the same. To leave the camp, you needed a civil pass. Neither of us had one. But we still put on our civies and headed for the gate. We were spotted by a sergeant who knew me fairly well. 'What are you doing in civies, McClelland? Go back and change and I'll get you a civilian pass tomorrow.'

We made as if to return to our billet, but as soon as he was out of sight, we legged it through the gate. Terry had a girlfriend, a WAC – meaning a female soldier. She was billeted at another barracks not so far from ours. That's where we headed, but when we got there, there was a sign up over the gate. 'No Rifle Brigade Allowed.'

Why? Because a few weeks earlier, not long after we'd finished basic training, we were all out and got very, very drunk on Scrumpy. On the way back to the barracks on the train, someone thought it would be a good idea to rip out the seats. Next thing you know, we were all at it. We destroyed the carriage – ripped everything out and fucked it out the door. It was a very strange thing, something I never did before and have never done since. Afterwards, we were all confined to barracks, and barred from every other billet.

But we didn't turn back. There was a dance that night, and Terry wanted to make sure his girlfriend would be there. While we were hanging around at the gate, trying to figure out what to do, two busses drove up. They were there to transport anyone who had a pass to the dance. I went up to the bus driver and told him we had girlfriends expecting to meet us, but that we had no passes. Would he help us out? He would. He told us to crouch down at the back. That's how we got off the base.

Terry met his girlfriend at the dance, and I met another girl and we had a few dances. Then who did I bump into? The sergeant who'd told me to change back into my uniform, the one who'd said he'd get me a civilian pass in the morning.

I don't think I ever saw anyone as angry. 'I'll have your fucking guts for garters McClelland.'

'Fuck off,' I told him, out of the side of my mouth.

'I'll see you in the morning,' he said.

But by then, myself and Terry were long gone.

I suppose I threw away what could have been a good career, but I had a bit of a temper, and I felt demeaned by that business with the buttons. The pettiness of it. I just couldn't bear to be treated that way. Maybe too that RSM had hit a bit of a sore spot. Ever since that man had called me a ragamuffin, I couldn't stand anyone passing remarks about my clothes.

Chapter 7
The Adventures of Rory McDarby

Terry had family from Spalding in Lincolnshire, so that's where we went. This area is very agricultural – big expanses of flat land. Batchelors have factories there and they grow a lot of peas and potatoes and that kind of thing. Everybody calls everybody else 'Duck'.

'Alright Duck?'

'Alright.'

Terry stayed with his mother. I stayed with his brother Cush, and his wife and two kids. One night, not long after I'd arrived, there was another friend of his staying there. He'd been a corporal in Winchester, but long before our time there. I didn't know him at all.

I didn't have a bed, just two fireside chairs pushed together. I woke up at one point and my legs were on the floor. The corporal had come in late and manoeuvred one of the chairs out from under me so he'd have a place to kip.

I said, 'You're after robbing half me bed.'

He started laughing. I was a bit nervy because I didn't know this fella at all, and of course he was still in the army and I was on the run. He turned out to be sound enough. He told me a story he'd heard from someone else in Winchester, about this mad Irishman who'd held them all up one night with his rifle. I changed the subject real fast.

I met a fantastic girl that weekend – June was her name. I would have liked to have stayed with her but both myself and Terry knew that it probably wasn't a good idea to hang around his home town. Far better to keep moving. Blackpool was of course a place I knew well, and there was nothing official to connect either myself or Terry with it, so that's where we headed next. We hitch-hiked most of the way, but had to sleep out one night in this little market town; I don't remember the name of it. A copper came and nudged me awake with his toe at some hour of the morning.

'What's your name?'

I was ready for this. I knew it would be a mistake to travel under my own name, so I'd made up a new one. It had to roll off the tongue fast, which is why I chose a name that wasn't a million miles from the real one.

'Rory McDarby.'

This cop's mother was Irish, and the minute he heard we were from the old sod, his attitude changed completely and we had a good old natter about Dublin.

'Finish your sleep and head off when you're ready.'

We got to Blackpool later that day, but that's where things went wrong for Terry. I had already thrown away my ID, but he wouldn't give up his. At that time, if you were a member of the armed forces, you never had to queue for anything. Flash the ID and every bouncer and doorman in the country – or most of them anyway – would stand aside and let you in.

We were sleeping out in this glass-covered area in front of the beach, where people would sit and look out at the waves. It was sheltered – which was great, but early one morning, not long after we arrived, I was half asleep when I heard someone say 'Ello, ello, ello?'

You only ever heard coppers say that in the pictures, but here was one saying it in real life.

I got to my feet quickly and gave him the same name I gave the other copper. 'Rory

McDarby'. This fella didn't have an Irish mother. He asked for ID.

'I don't have any, I'm just after coming over from Ireland. I got a job at The Dorchester on Queen's Promenade.' I rattled off their phone number from memory. I should say too that I never went near the Dorchester this time round. I could have gone there I suppose, and I'm sure the Yoxhalls would have welcomed me, but something kept me away. Maybe I was a little ashamed to be showing up a few years later in nothing but the clothes I stood up in.

Anyway, the copper asked Terry his name. You never saw a worse liar. 'F-f- Fred Shaw,' he stuttered.

'Who owns that bag?'

This was the bag with Terry's ID in it. The copper searched it and Terry was a goner.

'Why are you two together?' he asked me.

'I just met him a couple of hours ago,' I said.

That seemed to satisfy him. 'You can go,' he said to me, 'but you're coming with me *Fred*.'

Before I went off, Terry asked if he could give me his address so that I could write to him. The copper said ok, but before Terry passed me the slip of paper, the cop asked to see it. Of course this confirmed it, because he'd written his real name on it.

I wandered around for a couple of days before I found a job on the Golden Mile. This is the flashy part of Blackpool, where you'll find the funfair, the booths and shows and illuminations. I was a doorman at a casino, but it wasn't just a casino. There were restaurants and dancehalls and bars all in the one building. I did pretty well. I was still only seventeen but the army had toughened me up and I was fit and strong as a horse.

The only problem was that my boss, a German called Tommy Fosh, didn't really like me. One time, he came over to where I was working and pointed out this man who was hanging around the foyer. 'See him?' he said, 'throw him out.'

This guy was big – a good six inches taller than me, and very well built. 'Why d'you want to throw him out?' I said, 'he isn't causing any trouble.'

'Put him out!' he said.

So I went up to the fella and I said, 'Howaya, I'm Rory.'

'How are you doing Rory?'

I said, 'You see that little baldy fella over there? He's my boss, and he told me to put you out. You know and I know that I couldn't put you out, but would you go for me, just to spite the little bastard?'

Your man winked at me. 'I'll leave for you Paddy.'

As soon as he was gone, I looked over at Tommy, as if to say, *you happy now?*

But I knew my days were numbered there. Normally the Germans get on very well with the Irish, but this fella for some unknown reason had taken a dislike to me.

In the meantime, I got a letter from Terry. He ended up doing time in the military prison in Colchester, before being sent back to the regiment.

Did I worry that I'd get caught? Sometimes, yes. I was sitting in the window of the casino one day, admiring all the women going by when these two guys in suits arrived in.

'Are you Rory McDarby?'

'Yes.'

'You're due for national service.'

I nearly shit my trousers when I heard this. 'I'm only here a couple of months,' I protested, 'I'm only here for the season, I'm heading back to Ireland in September.'

'Then you'll have to come down to the office and sign a form to confirm that,' I was told.

I went down there afterwards, signed the form and got away with it.

I was on a break one evening, having a drink with another doorman, a Scottish fella, who'd also been in the army. The place was quiet, so he started showing me these gymnastic tricks that he'd learned. Flips and somersaults and things like this.

Same thing. Tommy comes up again and says, 'Send him home.'

'For fuck's sake, Tommy, he works here!' I said. 'He's not doing anything, just a few tricks.'

'Send him home!'

I said, 'You send him home.'

Tommy draws back and hits me a punch. That was it. I hit him back and next thing we were rolling around on the floor in front of these automatic doors – magic doors we used to call them. They kept opening and closing. Then the Scotsman jumped in and started in on me! And I was only defending him!

Someone pulled him off, he was taken upstairs and given the sack. Afterwards, he passed me by on the way out the door. He gave me a dirty look and said, 'I never liked Catholics anyway.'

Bitter oul bastard. That's the first experience I had of anything like that. Actually, no, now I think about it, Terry's girlfriend, the WAC I mentioned in the last chapter was one of those bitter Scottish Protestants too. She had a go at me for being a Catholic. Most people are grand, though, no matter where they're from.

Anyway, I thought I'd got away with the fight, but I got my cards the next day.

I stayed around the pleasure beach and got a job on the rifle range. I had to take the money and hand out the prizes and all that. And I had to do all the spieling: 'Step right up! Shoot for prizes!' Trying to drum up a bit of business. Sometimes, people would respond to the accent. 'Howaya Paddy!'

The money wasn't great, which is why I used to pocket some of the takings myself. If the boss had known, he'd probably have killed me. He was a man of small size from Lancashire named Harry Lancaster. He might have been small – and fairly old too – but he was all man. You wouldn't cross him. We used to share a taxi home in the evening, and he'd have to get out before me. He'd say to the taxi man, 'If lights are against thee, stop and let me out that side, if the lights are for thee, bring me to the far side.'

I remember one time, this guy came up to the rifle range. Well dressed, good looking man. He took his few shots and wandered off. Someone else who worked the stalls came over to me.

'You know who that was?'
'No.'
'It was Peter Manuel.'
'Who?'
'Peter Manuel, the killer.'

So it turned out that this guy was suspected of killing a number of people in Lanarkshire and Newcastle. I saw him again a few days later, and pointed him out to Harry, who was with me on the stall. Manuel had drink on him this time, and when he came back up to the rifle range, he started causing trouble – abusing some of the other customers. This was a mistake.

The rifles that we used were all chained to the front so no one could run off with them. Harry picked one of these up, unclipped it and hit your man into the side of the head with the butt of it. Knocked him out cold.

That same fella was tried for the murder of seven people in 1958. It was the talk of the country. He fired his lawyer and conducted his own defence, but he was convicted and they hanged him in Glasgow that summer.

I had this lovely flat downtown while I was in the casino, but I had to give it up after a while, I can't remember why. One of the men working the stalls told me to talk to Big Ronnie. He wasn't hard to find. He was huge. I mean huge. Six foot seven or eight, and almost as fat. Big baldy head on him. I talked to him anyway, and he said, yeah, he had a bed. He took me back to his place in a taxi that night, but as soon as we got there, I knew I'd made a mistake. I got the impression that Ronnie preferred boys to girls. I started talking about all the women I'd been with, to let him know that I wasn't that way inclined. I realised however that he didn't really give a shit what way I was inclined. I went to bed anyway, and when I woke up next morning, he was there at the bed with his hand down my pants. I jumped about a mile.

'Come on Rory,' he said, 'breakfast is ready.'

I got washed and dressed, then went in and ate the breakfast. I didn't want to; my stomach was turning, but I was afraid of him, to be honest, and didn't want to piss him off. I remember he said to me, 'I'll have you dressed better than the Duke of Edinburgh.'

In my own head, I said to myself, 'No you fuckin' won't.'

It was a Sunday morning, so I told him I had to go to mass. The perks of being a Catholic. I closed the door of Big Ronnie's flat and never went back. I even left stuff after me.

The pleasure beach didn't open till two on Sundays, so I wandered around all morning. Before I started work, I ran into the guy who'd suggested I go back to Big Ronnie's. He told me that he'd been in prison for molesting young men.

'Now you fuckin' tell me!' I said.

He felt so bad about it that he invited me to stay in his house until I got a place. I took him up on the offer, and ended up staying there quite a while. He had a wife and two boys – lovely young fellas – and we got on great together. The wife knitted me an Aran sweater afterwards. The only problem was that the breakfast was the same thing every single day: beans on bloody toast.

I also worked the racecourse stall. Here, the punters would have to roll these little balls up a shallow incline, and if you got one into the bucket, your dog would go forward a couple of inches. There were eight or nine other people sitting beside you trying to do the same thing. Whoever was the best at getting the balls into the buckets would get their greyhound across the line first and win a doll or a cuddly toy or something like that.

The great thing about working these stalls was the women. It was like you were a film star. Some nights, there'd be two girls waiting on me to finish. I've no idea why this was the case, but by God I made the most of it.

Working the racecourse stall, you were up on a height, so you could keep an eye on things and make sure no one was cheating and that. I was there one day, and who did I see in the crowd only my sister – my favourite sister – Martha. It was in the middle of a race, which meant I couldn't leave, so I started jumping up and down and waving. Then she looked up and saw me.

'You little pup!' she shouted. I laughed at that, because that's what Ma used to say to me all the time. 'Rory, you little pup!'

Martha came up and threw her arms around me. 'Mammy's looking for you everywhere!'

It had been a few months since I'd been home. 'How did you find me?' I asked her.

She said that she'd been to the casino and asked after me. She'd talked to a German girl who was in charge of serving ice-cream and Knickerbocker Glories and all that sort of stuff.

'I asked her if she knew you,' Martha said, 'and she said she didn't. But then as I was walking away, she called me back and asked if I was the little baby-faced fella.'

'Ah Jaysus!' I said. I didn't like to think of myself as a little baby-faced fella.

The whole time I was in Blackpool, I'd been writing to June – the girl I'd started going with in Spalding. I missed her, so I decided to pack it in and head back there. But when I arrived, I found out that she was on the game. So that was the end of that.

Like so many times in my life – before and since – I found myself at a loose end. I stayed with Cush and the family again. I liked his wife and I loved his two little kids, but the more I saw of Cush, the less I liked him. He was a bit of a wild man. He used to drink the family allowance. The children would often be hungry.

We got a job picking spuds with one of the big farmers. It was hard work – from 7AM till midday, but you got a fiver for the five hours, which was good money. Cush would go straight to the pub, but I'd go to the chipper, get two singles, two bits of fish and a portion of mushy peas. I'd take it all back to the house and eat with the kids and Paul. That was his wife's name. Short for Pauline I suppose.

I stayed there that Christmas, but it was lean times. We had almost nothing. So I went out with Cush late one night to see what we could find. There were all these little allotments just outside of town, including one with a chicken coop. Cush grabbed a hen but he hadn't the guts to wring its neck. I did. We brought it home and Paul got it ready and cooked it.

A few days later, they were bathing the kids in the living room. Paul was washing them in a basin on the floor and Cush was drying them on the table. The little girl was messing – she was only around four – and Cush gave her a wicked slap on the leg.

It was out of me before I could help it. 'There's no need for that.'

He didn't say anything but I knew he didn't like it. Later, after he'd been drinking, he started muttering to himself and looking over at me. I said, 'If you have something to say to me, fuckin' say it.'

He went off to bed, but I knew that my time in Spalding was up. I was sorry to say goodbye to Paul and the kids, but I'd nothing really keeping me there, and I'd worn out my welcome. So I hitch-hiked to Liverpool and took the boat for Dublin.

Chapter 8
Back in Uniform and Other Bad Decisions

I used to go to the Ritz in Ballyfermot for the dancing. I was there one time with a mate of mine, and felt someone pulling at the hairs on the back of my leg. I turned around and it was this young one. She went off, but then a little while later, I felt the same thing, turned around again and it was the same girl. This time I asked her to dance, and ended up leaving her home. She was from Drimnagh and her name was Eileen. We started going out together. It got quite serious quite quickly.

I ran out of money and wanted to go back to London. Eileen didn't want me to go, so we made a compromise. Instead of taking the boat, I'd join the army – the Irish army this time. I went down to Griffith Barracks to sign up, and was then assigned to another barracks further down the South Circular Road. Because I'd already been through basic training and knew how things worked, I found the whole set-up straight-forward and fairly effortless. Out on the parade ground, when they'd give the orders: *Left wheel! About face!* and all that, I knew exactly what to do. The sergeant would shout, 'Do what McClelland is doing!'

They used to call me Elvis, because I still had the haircut and the sideburns.

We got our jabs ahead of being sent abroad on peace-keeping. Can't remember exactly where it was they planned to send us, but we were told after getting the jab to avoid alcoholic drink, so I only had the one pint when I came out of the clinic, but there was this other recruit there – Ford was his name. Nice fella. He had a feed of pints and went nuts. Tried to jump out the window, four floors up. We had to drag him back in and put him to bed – and he was a big man. He kept making a run for the window to do it again, so we had to push all the beds together to fence him in.

It was while I was in the army that I met this guy. His first name was Ralph, and he told me he was a famous thief. Full of stories of the houses he had broken into and the things he had whipped out from under the noses of people. I was young, stupid and impressionable, and this fella impressed me. He convinced me to meet up with him one night to go rob a house, but he never showed up. I remember standing there in the dark and suddenly starting to see sense.

'What are you doing here?' I said to myself.

There wasn't a huge difference between the two armies – same kind of drilling, same kind of billets, same kind of food, same kind of rifles – Lee Enfields. You got neither ammunition nor grenades in the Irish Army. But the biggest difference was the money. In the British Army, you got a fiver a week. In the Irish Army, you only got two pounds and fourteen shillings. The other problem was that you had to be back in the barracks at midnight. This didn't suit me at all. I thought I'd still be able to go to the Ritz, I thought I'd be able to buy clothes and have a few quid to spend. Plus I'd done it all before, I was bored and I wanted out again.

Getting out of the army is not easy. There was one lad there, he was a great runner, and twice while I was in the barracks, he ran away. Both times he got hauled back.

So I made an appointment to see the CO. Up in his office, he said, 'What can I do for you McClelland?'

'Sir, I want to leave the army. I can't afford to give my mother anything and I'm a bit of an alcoholic.' I let on to have a shake. 'I can't concentrate properly when I haven't got a drink.'

'And how many pints would you drink of an evening?' he asked.

'Ten or eleven sir.' I was still only a scrawny young fella. There'd be no way I could drink anything like that.

He told me to go back to the billet and that he'd let me know. The next day, I got my release. I'd been in the army exactly eighty-eight days.

This time I put the foot down and said I was going to London. Eileen said, 'Fair enough, but I'm coming with you.'

The first few weeks, we stayed with my brother Gerry and his wife Eithne. They were living in a kind of hostel for people who couldn't get accommodation anywhere else. The place had been a school at one point, and it was fairly rough. These slim partitions divided one flat from the next, so there wasn't much privacy.

I remember being out in the kitchen one night. There were a few people visiting and

Eithne says to them, 'You remember I was telling you about that fella who ran away from the army? Well, this is him.'

'Jaysus Eithne,' I said, 'thanks very much!'

Going back to London was risky. I was still on the run. If I was found, they'd lock me up in Colchester and throw away the key. That's why, while I was over there, I was never 'Rory'. I called myself Alan.

I always liked Eithne though. She was always dead straight. But it was a bit awkward living on top of each other like that. We had no space for ourselves. It was Eithne herself who solved the problem. She found myself and Eileen a place each over on the far side of the city. This was 1959 and we were unmarried. We might have been away from home, but Eithne didn't like the fact that we were living together and no ring on Eileen's finger. My place was in Camberwell, up on the fifth floor of one of those old London houses. It was still very basic – no toilet, no cooking facilities, but I had the room to myself, and the landlord, Chris, and his wife Vera were lovely people. They lived on the ground floor. Eileen's place didn't work out for one reason or another. She ended up moving in with me.

I got a job in the London Oil Corporation, lugging sixteen-stone bags of lard and emptying them into this big cauldron. It was very heavy work but I was fit as fiddle and it didn't knock anything out of me. I remember I made friends with a scouser called Eddie. He came in one morning, miserable and I asked him what was wrong. He told me that he'd had sex with his girlfriend for the first time the night before, and that he'd packed her in.

'Why did you pack her in?' I said.

'Because if she'd let me, she'd let anyone.'

'For fuck's sake', I said, 'get a grip on yourself. You're two adults, and women have feelings the same as we do. She obviously loves you. Go straight back to her.'

He did, and he was a much happier man because of it. But that was the kind of thing you learned back then: that a woman who'd have sex with you was no good.

I left that job after a bit and applied for a cleaning job in a cake factory: Daisy Fresh Cakes. As part of the hiring process, I had to fill out a form, and when the woman interviewing me looked at it, she said, 'Are you a pastry chef?'

'Oh yeah,' I said, 'I am.'

I didn't know what a pastry chef was, but I'd said on the form that I'd been a chef's assistant in The Dorchester in Blackpool. Now, the Dorchester in Blackpool had nothing whatsoever to do with the Dorchester on Park Lane, which was one of poshest hotels in the world. I'm not sure if your one mixed them up, but it was the fact that I'd been a chef of any sort that caught her eye.

She said, 'I've a job for you. It'll be available in a month. I'll put you on the cleaning staff until then.'

That cleaning job was actually great crack. I was working with these two guys, Georgie and Jamie. About a month in, I was brought up to meet the manager and shown around the factory. I was told I'd be making almond slices – but in bulk. This turned out to be a great little number. I had two men working under me doing all the lifting and carrying. I said to them, 'Just don't fuck about lads and we'll all get on.'

There were big sacks of sugar and five gallon drums full of shelled eggs. You had to pour these, in the right proportions, into a sort of cement mixer, and when the texture was right, you'd pour the mixture onto these trays. A set of conveyor belts and rollers took them off to be cut and baked and the rest of it. It was a good job, and I was fairly handy at it – I never once had a batch rejected.

Eileen meanwhile got a job in a factory that made amp-meters: the things that measure electrical current. But she the jealous type, Eileen, and she insisted that I give up the almond slices and come and work with her. As far as she was concerned, there were too many good-looking women where I was.

Why did I give up a job I liked? Where I was doing well and making decent money? I'm a man that likes peace.

But she got pregnant and I decided I'd have to do my duty by her. I was only nineteen, and at that time, if you were under twenty-one, you had to get permission from a parent before you could get married. I wrote home to my mother but she refused. So I wrote to Lily, and she got around ma. I remember the day the letter arrived telling me I could go ahead and tie the knot.

I don't know if I was ever really in love with Eileen. She loved me, I knew that, and that made all the difference. The years of poverty and shame had left their mark. I might have been well able to act tough, but inside, my self esteem was on the ground. I got it into my head that no one else would have me. So we stayed together for a long time – far too long, probably. We were never suited. By then, I had a string of bad decisions behind me, from abandoning my coat in a toilet to abandoning two armies and any number of jobs.

We were both sending money home – me to my ma, her to hers. If the money was a bit short, Eileen would say to me 'Don't send anything to your ma this week,'

My ma was a widow. My wife's da was still alive.

We needed two witnesses to get married, so I asked a fella out of my job to come along the Saturday morning, and Eileen asked someone from her job, but both of them let us down, so we got Chris and Vera to come instead. Fair play to them, they were happy to do it. Chris bought a bottle of champagne and we had a bit of a party with a few of the neighbours back at the flat, then he gave me two pounds and told me to take my wife into the West End and go to the pictures. We saw a Kirk Douglas movie. I can't think of the name of it.

    I was earning good money in London, I didn't want to leave, but she was anxious to get back to Dublin again, so we packed it in, gave up the room and headed for Liverpool.

Chapter 9
Finger Tips

The big question, when we got back home, was where we'd stay. Eileen was about to have the child, but there was no room in my mother's. Lily had moved out and got her own place by then, but my other sister, Anne, had moved in with her family.

So we moved in with Eileen's mother and father in Drimnagh. It was crowded, and we weren't the most welcome house guests. There were several – I'll call them arguments. Despite that, my mother-in-law was a lovely woman. I always liked her, and she was always very close to my kids. I'd sometimes borrow a few quid off her.

'Will you give it back to me, Rory McClelland?' she used to say.

'Don't I always pay you back?'

I met this woman's mother too – Eileen's grandmother. She had a flat in Dorset Street and lived to be ninety-six. I remember she had a head of pure white hair and a beautiful face. This was a woman who was born in and around

1870. We got on great together. I used to bring her bottles of stout.

'Will you go downstairs, Rory, and get me a small glass of whiskey. Tell him it's for Mrs. Deegan and he'll give you a good measure.'

My sister Martha found us a room to rent on Moran Road in Drimnagh – that's where we were when Vincent was born in July 1960.

I had a lot of trouble finding a job. I was going round factories all day and didn't have a bob. I wasn't just young, I looked young, and that didn't work in my favour. I met this guy somewhere, I don't remember where, and he told me where there was a job going, but wanted a fiver just for telling me.

'You'll be getting good money,' he said.

'Wait till I see what I'll be getting,' I said.

The job was with a builder, but he'd only give me a fiver a week, so I told your man he was getting nothing.

We were doing up a house in Phibsborough that was owned by a copper. I was still terrified of coppers; I used to be afraid to use the toilet in the house, and pissed in the bin in the shed instead. In fairness to the man, he was kind to me – maybe too kind. He used to give me cabbage from the garden to bring home to Eileen. I learned a lot on that job: bricklaying and roofing, I cut out plasterboard and studded out the ceiling. The builder showed me what to do and I did it. But then the copper asked me how much the builder was paying me. I suppose he wasn't too happy with what the builder was charging him. When my employer found out that I told the copper I was only getting a fiver a week, he sacked me. So that was the end of that.

After that, I found a job in Lamb's Jam factory, then in the Woolen Mills on the Long Mile road. Hard work, heavy work, boring work.

I was working overtime one Saturday morning. I finished up at midday and thought about going for a pint, but in the end decided against it. I heard the screaming as soon as I opened the front door. My wife had the landlady by the throat. I ran to pull her off and ended up on the ground with the two of them on top of me. It took a while to calm Eileen down and find out what happened. It turned out that someone had taken the brake off the pram, and my wife decided that it was the landlady. The child wasn't even in it at the time.

Eileen got taken to court, and I was called as a witness.

'In your own words Mr. McClelland, tell me what happened.' So I told him what I knew, which wasn't anything more than I've just written here. Eileen didn't give evidence but the landlady did. She tried to make out she was a harmless little old lady, but I remember the judge said to her, 'I imagine you have your moments, madam.'

Eileen ended up getting off anyway, but a few weeks later she arrived up to me in work and said that our furniture was all out in the front garden. We'd been evicted. It was hardly a surprise.

We went back to Eileen's mother, who said, 'Leave the baby with me until you find a place.' Herself and myself ended up in a tramp's hostel in town for a couple of weeks. There was a women's side and a men's side. By Jesus, that place was miserable.

So I went to see my sister Lily, and she agreed to give us a room in her house in Ballyfermot. Her husband wasn't too happy to see us coming, but he was glad to live in our house for years, so he could put up with us for a while.

Lily's box room was tiny, cold and damp. The only place for the baby to sleep was on my chest. At the time, I was working one of two shifts: 7AM to 3PM or 3PM to 11PM. Then Lily's husband started laying down the law.

'You have to be in by midnight.'

I had to explain to him that if I was on the late shift, there was no way I'd get home before twelve.

We couldn't wait to get out of there, but what we found next wasn't much better. A room down in Keogh Square, just off the South Circular Road. This place used to be Richmond Barracks before the War of Independence – the British Army were stationed there back then. It was converted into living accommodation afterwards, but by the sixties, the place was run down and in need of attention. There was more room here, but there was no running water and to get to the toilet upstairs, you had to get past the landlady, who didn't make life easy for us. In the end I gave up and just went out to the canal to go to the toilet.

And the place was overrun with mice. I put cement down along the edge of the floor and in all the little holes and nooks and crannies, but they ate through that, so I mixed crushed glass in with the cement and that did the trick.

I drifted between jobs for a while, then my sister Anne's husband, Paddy, got me a place in CB Sacks. They made paper bags of all sorts.

But Eileen used to resent any time I wasn't at home. In particular, she hated when I worked overtime, but I was trying to make a bit of money for the family. You couldn't refuse time and a half.

I was assistant machine man in that factory, and when the head machine man got promoted, I was in line for his job. But another lad – Bob was his name – was better connected than I was, and even though he'd only been in the place a couple of months and hadn't been properly trained, he got the job over me. He was working this machine called a stepper. You feed in the paper and it cuts it and glues it and a finished cement bag pops out the other end. Before I took on the job, the machine was producing 100,000 sacks an hour, but I figured out a way of getting that up to 120,000 an hour. This new guy however didn't know what he was doing and ended up losing two of his fingers to the machine.

That meant I got his job 'by process of elimination' as the foreman put it. I did not like this man. There was a cruel streak in him. I remember him boasting that he had shot a duck, sitting on her nest when she was surrounded by her little ducklings. He did other things that I'm not going to talk about here.

If the paper in the stepper got torn, you had to repair it by putting in new paper by hand. One morning anyway, not long after Bob had his accident, I had to replace the paper, so I turned the machine off and got the assistant machine man to stand ready to hit the button at my word. So I'm down feeding the paper in and the foreman walks by, pushes my assistant out of the way and hits the button on the machine when I'm not expecting it. My right hand gets caught in the rollers, I felt a sudden tug and wrenched my arm away. I didn't want to look at it, but I looked at it. The middle and ring finger of my right hand were bloodied. I couldn't see nails on either of them.

I wriggled out from under the machine, cradling my mangled hand. The assistant rushed over. 'Are you ok?'

'Am I fuck?' I could see the foreman grinning at me, the prick.

'Show me,' said the assistant.

'It's after taking the tops of my fingers off.'

'Let's see.'

'No.' I didn't want to look at it myself.

'Let's see.'

'Here.'

When he saw what the machine had done, he fainted.

The strange thing was, it wasn't sore, not at first. For some reason, they didn't want to call an ambulance, but nor did anyone want to drive me. Why? Because they'd seen enough of these accidents to know how it worked. When the shock wears off, the pain arrives, and it's so bad, you grab the person nearest to you, and that's often the fella that's driving the car. People had crashed in these situations.

They got a fella to drive me in anyway. 'Rory,' he said, 'don't fuckin' touch me if the pain kicks in.'

As it turned out, the pain did kick in in the car. It was fucking excruciating, but I didn't grab your man, I didn't touch him. We got down to Steeven's Hospital there opposite Heuston Station – the same place my mother used to bring me when I was a kid. They gave me an injection, thank God, and the pain settled down a bit. Then I was taken in and examined. In the end, they had to take skin off my arse to repair the fingers, and they did a decent job, though the nails were gone for good.

They gave me another injection before I left, but it had worn off by that evening. I'll never forget the pain. I was banging my head off the headboard it was so bad.

Back then, accidents like this were common enough in factories. I knew one man who had his head taken off by a printing press.

I was eleven weeks out of work, living off five pound a week from the workman's compensation fund. They did a collection for me at work too, but here again the foreman had another dirty trick up his sleeve. They'd collected for Bob the week before, but because he hadn't been in the place long, and wasn't well liked, they didn't manage to get very much for him. So the foreman decided not to give Bob anything until after my collection was taken up. I'd been in the place a couple of years, and everyone knew me, so they were generous, fair play to them, but the foreman combined the two collections and divided it in two. Bob was only a young fella, he had no kids, but at that stage I had two kids at home. I could have done with that money.

We had several neighbours in Keogh Square. One of them was a bit famous. He was a great singer – they used to call him Ireland's Elvis Presley – I remembered seeing him at the Hollywood Club in Highbury back when I was in London. There was another fella though who was a right prick. I won't give his name here. I wasn't long home from the hospital, I still had my arm in a sling and was talking to Elvis on the stairs. He was all sympathy over what had happened. Your man – for no reason other than jealousy that Elvis was talking to me – drew back and gave me a head-butt that broke my nose and landed me on my back on the floor. I had to go back to the hospital again to get that sorted out. Now I think of it, this was actually the second time I'd had my nose broken. Years earlier, when I was a kid, a fella accidentally hit me with a hurley. That left a dent on my nose. Some fella told me I looked like Joe Louis. I was delighted with myself.

Anyway, a few years after the accident at work I was in a pub down in the docks – Mulvihils. Fairly rough spot. I noticed the man who'd head-butted me drinking by himself just inside the door. I was up at the bar when the barman says, 'I never noticed your broken nose before Rory.'

I knew that your man had been boasting, so I said, loud enough for the whole place to hear, 'The man who told you he broke my nose didn't tell you that my arm was in a sling at the time, or that I was after getting the tops off my fingers a couple of days before that.'

The good news is that with the money I got for losing the tops of my fingers – £560 – I bought a car. An Austin Farina. It was great. For a while, we thought we were rich.

We had four kids in Keogh Square, and though it never got easy, we did have some fun there. I used to get down on the floor with them and we'd have play fights. We used to watch the dog racing on the TV and bet on it amongst ourselves. They'd be crying if their dog lost. We got a gas stove to make food on, but we never had water. We had to wash the kids in a basin, and I used to go to my sister's for a shower. I don't know how we managed. Going up and down the canal looking for a place to go to the toilet. Terrible.

Chapter 10
Hard Times, Hard Men

I was seven years in CB Sacks. When I went back after the accident, they put me working in the store, managing the stock of paper, driving a forklift and all that. I also put my name forward as shop steward and ended up doing quite a lot of union work. There was one day I came in for my shift and the place was in silence. Everyone was after downing tools.

The factory was right next door to Clondalkin Paper Mills. At one time, CB Sacks and the paper mill had actually been the same company, and though they were separate now, there was still a close relationship between the two. The mill supplied a lot of the paper we used, in particular the cement sacks that I made. They were out on strike for one reason or another at this time, and their strike committee had asked us not to substitute imported paper for their paper in the manufacture of the cement bags. Fair enough we said, and we wrote to management to let them know that we had this agreement. They never challenged it, but now, when they couldn't get paper next door, they used imported paper. The assistant shop steward – who was on the shift before me – said, 'Right, that's it, they're using imported paper. Strike on here.'

The manager there was a bit of an antique. He'd always looked down his nose at us. Now he decided that he'd lock us out.

Fair enough. Out we went. We requested a delegate from union HQ to make the whole thing official, but we knew we had them dead to rights. A meeting was held between ourselves and management, with the union delegate as well – though he wasn't much use to be honest. Management conceded they were wrong, and that they shouldn't have substituted foreign paper for local paper. It was a stupid thing to be striking over. These men all had families, they loved their jobs and up to this point, we had great relationships with management. We lost a week and a half's pay over a stupid strike.

'We could have avoided all this,' I said to the manager, 'If you had honoured your own commitments. Would it not be more conducive to good relations if you treated us with a bit of respect?'

Anyway, it was at CB Sacks that I got into bagatelle. This is a game that you never see anywhere anymore, but if was fairly popular in Dublin in the early sixties. You play with cues and balls like snooker or billiards. There are holes at one end of the table, with mushrooms in front of them, and the aim of the game is to get the balls into holes without knocking over these mushrooms. We had a good team in Vaughan's pub, and won the league one year. They called it the 7-Up Cup. We had a lot of craic at it, and put in a lot of time going out to other clubs and pubs playing the game.

After a couple of years working in the store, I got to know it inside out, to the point where I was able to put out enough paper for the whole shift in a couple of hours. This meant that if I was on from three till eleven, I'd have all of the machines stocked by seven. So that's when I used to go missing, and just get someone in the factory to ping me out at eleven. I'd been doing that for months, no problem, when I met a woman at a soccer match one Sunday morning. She told me that the previous Friday night, they were short a thousand bags for a particular order, but when they went looking for me to get the paper, they couldn't find me. I'd left at 7PM, same as usual, to go to a bagatelle match.

'Oh right,' I said to her, 'thanks for the information.'

As it turned out, my father in law died that Monday, and because there was no one else around to manage things, I took care of the arrangements. That kept me busy for a couple of days, then I got my cards in the post.

I was earning decent money in that job, but I knew I'd pick up another one easy enough. And I did: in Chapelizod a few days later. Another paper factory. The machine they put me on was antiquated – it took me a couple of days to find my way around it, but then it was grand. The manager however wasn't grand. Another snob. He sent for me one day. Now back then, I smoked – and back then, you were allowed smoke anywhere, even a paper factory – which is madness when you think about it. I had a fag between my fingers when I walked into the manager's office.

'I didn't give you permission to come in here smoking.'

'Do you smoke in here?' I asked him.

'Yes, but—'

'Well what's the difference between you and me?'

He said, 'I'm the manager.'

'Your attitude is all wrong mate.'

He stared at me for a minute, then said, 'I'm afraid I'll have to let you go.'

'Well,' I said, 'you can give me two weeks' pay in lieu of notice. I left a job to come here.'

This wasn't exactly true, but he didn't know that.

So he gave me the two weeks' pay. I'd only been in the place a couple of weeks. Three days later, I had a job down at the docks, driving a forklift.

It was a strange kind of a direction to take. Up until this point, I'd stayed around the places that I knew: Inchicore, Clondalkin, Ballyfermot. I'd never been anywhere near the docks. And to be honest I was a bit nervous, because the place had a violent reputation. There'd been a murder down there a few years earlier – it had been all over the papers. The main reason I went was because someone had seen me operating the roller clamp that we used to move paper rolls around and told me that I'd do well on the docks.

But this was very different from working in a nice warm factory. I was out in the open in all weathers. Nobody used raingear. It was freezing when it wasn't wet, and wet when it wasn't freezing and sometimes it was both. And dangerous? Jesus Christ.

The guy who owned the operation was a character. Ted Shanahan was his name. He had a big boozer's nose but never drank in his life. He was a great boss – more of a mate than a manager. We all used to hang around in the office when we were taking breaks. When he was getting married, he brought every man to a hotel in town and we had a great night of free drink and singsongs. And he brought us to the wedding too. Couple of big tables down in one corner. In his speech, he said, 'Do you see that crowd of men over there? None of you would be here if it wasn't for them.'

He knew how to look after people, he knew how to run a business without looking down his nose at anyone.

We might have been working on the docks, but we weren't dockers, not the in the strict sense. We worked for Ted's company driving forklifts – doing all the heavy work to be perfectly honest about it. The dockers would all hang around the door of the shed, you'd have to bip them to get them out of the way. I used come up behind them and slam the forks down onto the ground to give them a fright. Their nerves would be bad from the drink and they'd nearly jump out of their skins.

'Oh Jesus!'

They had all nicknames: Funnier, Mick the Pill, Shoulders, Rasher, Jazzer. Funnier in particular had terrible bad nerves from the drink. You'd creep up behind him and roar and he'd jump a mile into the air.

Employment practices among the dockers were kind of unusual. They were casual labour. If there was a boat coming in, a Stevedore, who was an agent for a shipping line, would stand up on the platform and call out the names of all the dockers who'd been picked to work that job. Some of these boats were big – it could take a week to load or unload them. The dockers themselves were divided into button men and men who had no button. If you had a button, you had your pick of the work – it was like a union card. These fellas got jobbed first, then the other dockers got whatever was left. How did you get a button? It was handed down from father to son.

Dockers made good money, but as far as I could see, it was us – the forklift men – that did all the work. I said to one of them one time. 'See that?' I held out my index finger.

'What?'

'If you lose that, you're fucked. You'll never be able to work again.'

'What?'

'All you do is point. Move that here, move that there – directing the forklifts where to go.'

He didn't find that amusing.

If a lorry came in to collect a twenty-foot container, or you had the take a container off a lorry, you'd need four forklifts – one at each corner, all working in perfect harmony. As you were raising the container, you had to keep your foot hard on the brake to stop the back of the forklift from tipping up. I was a couple of years in the place when the guy lifting alongside of me started to panic. The weight of the container under the forks put the arse of the forklift up in the air.

'Keep your fuckin' foot on the brake!' I roared. If he didn't, he could shoot backwards and the container would come down on top of me. There'd be no point in bringing me to the hospital after that. They'd have to scrape me off the concrete.

This way of lifting was very dangerous and totally illegal, but that was the way it was back then. There was a fella killed on the forklifts while I was there. He was coming across the docks and hit an oil slick as he was turning. The whole thing toppled over and landed on him. Paddy Rogers was his name; I'll never forget it.

Later on, Ted bought a side loader, which made the whole business a lot safer. You could pull up beside the lorry, the forks would go under the container and you could either load it onto the train or the boat, or you could take it onto the back of the loader and use it as a lorry.

Another time, we were unloading a boat at the North Wall and I had two boxes, each a ton weight, stacked on the forks and was bringing them into the shed to put them up on the racks. Next thing one of the dockers comes running across the yard, waving his hands and roaring. There was always so much slagging and joking going on that it would have been easy for me to ignore him, but I didn't, and it was a good thing I didn't.

'Stop!' he was shouting, 'Stop! Stop.'

I was halfway in the door of the shed, but stopped and looked up to where he was pointing. There was a bar that ran across the top of the doorway, and as I was moving in through it, this bar had pushed the topmost box backwards so that it was teetering there on its edge. If I'd gone a couple of inches further, it would have tipped over on top of me and I would have been mashed. There were no hoods on those forklifts, no protection at all. When I think how close I came to a quick and violent death, I get a cold shiver down my back. I reversed very quickly, then jumped down and threw my arms around your man. He had saved my life.

Others weren't so lucky. I had one particular friend, Jimmy McCain. He was what you called the gear man. He worked down in the gear shed and if you needed tools or special equipment, that's where you went to get it. 'Rory, go down to the gear shed and get me the sister hooks.' These were the four chains – each with a hook on the end – that you hung off the crane's big hook if you wanted to lift, say, a pallet of fertiliser bags. We used to handle an awful lot of fertiliser. If a bag split, it would send this stuff everywhere: into your eyes, into your mouth. We were working on land that was reclaimed from the sea, don't forget, and it was always windy down there.

So Jimmy knew the job inside and out, and he was a lovely fella. Everyone loved him. He was down in the lower hold of a boat one morning when they were stacking these huge rolls of paper. They had them almost up to the roof when the whole lot collapsed. The row on the bottom burst outwards and ran over him, killing him instantly. Terrible.

Despite the dangers, everyone preferred to work inside the boat because you got an extra two quid an hour. Dangerous work, because the deck could be wet and slippery. A couple of times I got into a skid and had to jam the mast of the forklift against the roof to stop.

The cranes that sat all along the North Wall would lift the forklift down into the hold of the ship, and you'd work away in there, lifting the stuff up and out. It could be tricky, especially loading. You had to make sure that the containers were steady and secure on the deck. The sailors would lash them down afterwards, but they had to be even and tight otherwise they'd come lose out at sea and could tip the ship over.

Stuff would get damaged all the time. Not always by accident. One time, I was in the Point Depot. It's a concert venue now, but back then, it was where all of CIE's trains would terminate. You had everything from mail to cattle coming through there. I was heading off on the forklift when one of the dockers asked me to come over to where they had this huge barrel of beer. About six foot tall and the same again wide.

'Give that a nudge there,' he said.

I knew exactly what he meant, so I reversed the forklift, took aim and stabbed the barrel right at the base. Beer erupted out of the gash I'd made. They all had mugs at the ready and they zeroed in on this hole and started filling them up and drinking the beer down as fast they could.

Stuff got robbed too. I was never that good at robbing, not half as good as some of the others, but I did it.

One time, I was down in the lower hold and I took this lovely transistor radio. When the crane came to lift the forklift out, I stayed on the saddle and hid the radio on my lap. I made it out of the boat ok, but that didn't mean anything. You could very easily get stopped at the gate by the Customs and Excise men, so I showed the radio to one of the lads in the yard.

'Jesus, that's lovely,' he said, 'how much do you want for it?'

'Twenty quid.'

'Twenty quid?'

I said, 'Look at it! It's the dog's bollix!'

He gave me the twenty quid and went off. A couple of weeks later he came back to me.

'I'm in trouble Rory. You know that radio you sold me? I gave a present of it to a fella, it broke down and he brought it into the agent and they told him it was stolen.'

Shit.

I was the shop steward at the time, so I went and talked to Ted. He said, 'I'll tell you what. We'll say that someone found it, but we couldn't find the owner, so I put the value of it into the sick fund, and gave a present of it to your man.'

That's the story we gave, and we got away with it.

Another day I was back at the Point Depot, loading cartons of whiskey onto a boat. I said to myself, 'I'll have one of these', so when there was no one looking, I stashed a carton in a corner of the shed. When I finished loading, I went back and put it on the floor of the forklift. I was shitting myself as I went up the yard, but I sailed through the Customs checkpoint.

Lovely.

I went straight to my car, put the carton in the boot and threw an old raincoat over it.

That evening when I went home, I didn't bother taking it out of the car. I had my dinner and then went out to a bagatelle match. Afterwards, I was coming home up Bowe Lane, which is all zig zag, turning one way then the other. I was halfway up when I heard the *beebaw, beebaw* and saw the blue light flashing in the mirror.

'Oh fuck.'

I pulled in, the cop pulled in behind me and came up to the window. 'You were driving very erratically there,' he said.

I argued with him for bit before he asked me to get out and open the boot. Shite. I got out and was about to open it when his mate shouted at him from the car. They'd got another call and had to leave in a hurry. Couldn't believe my luck.

I hurried home, took the carton out and carried it into the house. That's when I found out. It wasn't whiskey at all. It was fucking bubblegum. I knew that I was loading both, but I thought I'd taken the whiskey. I hadn't.

You could get in a lot of trouble for taking things from the boats. Losing your job was only the start of it. There was a story in the paper around that time about a haulier who took four oranges from a boat. Four lousy oranges. He got stopped on the way out by Customs and Excise and they arrested him – they've the power to do that – and stuck him in a cell. But they never took the oranges off him, so he ate the four of them – skin and all. The headline in the paper was, 'Father of Four Eats the Evidence'.

There was another day, my forklift was broken down and Ted asked me to take the little works van down to the far end of the port to do a job – I don't remember what. Afterwards, I was sitting in it having a smoke when all of a sudden I felt myself being lifted up. 'Jaysus!' I grabbed onto the seat as the whole thing wobbled into the air. I pulled open the door, but by then I was too high up to jump, and I could hear the laughing from the ground. Next thing the van was carried forward and settled on top of a container. I opened the door again, but it was a sheer drop. They'd sneaked up on me and used the side loader to put me up on top of the container. There was fuck all I could do about it, I could go nowhere. The bastards left me up there half the day before they let me down again.

We drank all the time: before work, during work, after work. The pubs would be packed at seven in the morning. There was a time when I needed four large whiskeys to stop the shakes in the morning – and I wasn't the only one. I was dying of a hangover this particular day. Someone was after robbing a crate of port. I hated port, but I needed the cure, so I drank it. Another time, I had the shakes very bad but had nothing to take the edge off. I asked one of the checkers if he did, but all he had was a bottle of that yellow stuff: Advocaat. I drank every last drop.

We used to drink in the pub across from the Abbey Theatre: The Flowing Tide. You'd often meet the stars coming in there – Milo O'Shea was one of them. They mixed easy with us, they weren't snobby. People in the theatre know what it's like to be hungry.

But I'd turned into a hard drinker. If I only drank four pints before going home, I'd be clapping myself on the back.

Chapter 11
Around the Houses

About 1964, we finally got a corporation flat on Benburb Street and were able to leave Keogh Square, but it wasn't much of a step up to be honest about it. A ground floor flat, but divided in two, with the second half across the hall. There was a homeless shelter for single men attached to our building, and the area had become a bit of red-light district. From the back of our flat, you could see into a lane where they'd be going at it at all hours of the day. One time, my wife was hanging up the washing and an oul fella waved a pound at her and asked her if she'd come down to him. I went into Dublin Corporation to complain. 'Why can't you give me a decent house?'

'You came from a second class dwelling, so you're only going to get a second class dwelling.'

At least it had water and a bathroom.

At the time, you had to spend six months in any corporation house before you could apply for a transfer, and at that point, the best way to get one was by finding someone who'd do a straight swap with you. So when we had the six months served in Benburb Street, I put an ad in the paper looking for a place in Clondalkin, Ballyfermot, Inchicore or anywhere around there, but the only answer I got was from a guy in Finglas. I didn't really know Finglas. They had a pub there – Bottom of the Hill – that had a bagatelle table; I'd played there a few times. But we weren't getting any more offers, and anything was better than a divided flat in an area that didn't have much going for it so we said we'd try Finglas for six months. In fairness, it was a step up from Benburb Street. The neighbours were good, but it was a hell of a drive over to work in Clondalkin, and to be honest about it, I didn't really consider Finglas to be Dublin at all. As far as I was concerned, it was like going back to England. It was a foreign place to us. I couldn't wait to get back to Dublin from the north side, not least because I missed the pubs of Inchicore.

So again, we waited the six months, then put another ad in the paper, and this time, we struck lucky. I got a reply from a fella who lived on Rialto Road. Only he never put down which number house, and he never gave a phone number. Rialto Road is a long road, but I walked the length of it and knocked on every door – it took a full day. I never found him, so nothing came of that.

One night, I got back from my shift and Eileen was out at the shops. I had something to eat and fell asleep on the couch. Then the kids shook me awake.

'Dad! Dad! There's two nuns at the door.'

I got up and went out to them. First thing they said to me: 'Is your daddy at home?'

I knew I was young-looking, but surely I wasn't that young-looking. 'I'm the daddy,' I said.

They were selling first aid kits. I liked the look of them so I ordered one. As I was walking back into the room, I caught sight of myself in the mirror. While I was asleep, the kids had coloured in my face with black marker. I looked like one of those minstrels in the old movies. Needless to say, I never heard from those nuns again.

Eventually, one of my ads paid off. I got a reply from a fella called Minogue in Ballyfermot. He left a phone number, thank God, so I called him up, then I went down and met himself and his wife. Lovely people. The Minogues were happy to head for Finglas, and I was delighted to be able to come back to Ballyfermot and the pubs I knew. We moved into Claddagh Road and spent twelve great years in that house. It's the place my kids consider home more than any other.

I used to drink in Vaughan's in Inchicore, which was owned by Mick Vaughan. Him and his brother did very well, they had various pubs and houses and land all around the place.

Mick was a gas man. There was a fella used to come into the pub – Georgie – who drove a big tar lorry, and one day, Mick robbed it for the craic. He hid it down the hill and around the corner in a little lane, then came back up to the pub. When Georgie saw the lorry gone, he went mad looking for it. But Georgie got his own back in the end. When Mick made another attempt to take the lorry, Georgie and two of his mates trapped him in the cab, took off his shoes and socks, drove down to Kilmainham and kicked him out. Then they rang the cops and told them there was a mad man on the loose in Kilmainham.

There was a big country boy who worked in Vaughan's – Tom Nevin. From Galway. Lovely fella. We used to play bagatelle for chickens on a Friday night and darts for chickens on Sundays. Tom was the kind of fella that if he won a chicken, he'd give it to someone who wasn't working and needed it more than he did. One of good ones, Tom. I'd meet him from time to time over the years. He bought a pub in Finglas after, and I went out there to see him. He came out from behind the bar and we had great chat that day.

I didn't hear of him for years until the news came that he'd been murdered in the pub he'd bought in Wicklow – Jack White's. Of course it came out in the trial that it was his wife had done it. She tried to hire fellas to shoot him, but they ended up giving evidence against her in the trial. I found the whole thing terribly upsetting.

Anyway, later on, when business was going well, I bought a big house in Inchicore. It was on St. Vincent's Street, and backed onto the Goldenbridge Convent. It had six bedrooms, but needed a lot of work. I stripped out the inner part first, replastered and rewired, then built a porch on the front. I also put on a new roof, and built a lovely annex out the back, with red brick inside and crystal light fittings along the wall. It was a great job, we were all delighted with it. I also did away with one of the bedrooms and put in a workshop there instead. At the time, I had a fella working for me, and he had two dogs – a Jack Russell and a kind of collie mixed with I don't know what. This fella didn't treat the dogs very well, and when it came time for him go home, the collie wouldn't go with him. He wouldn't leave. My kids took him in and Prince became our dog. He was just gorgeous and the smartest dog you ever met. I used to sit on the armchair and say, 'I love Prince!' and he'd jump up on the chair and start licking and kissing me. Then I'd say, 'I hate dogs!' and he'd get down on the carpet and cover his face with his paws. '...but I love Prince!' and he'd jump back on top of me again. Amazing dog.

We hadn't much of a back garden because I used it as a kind of work yard, but it looked out on the back of the canal, and people would take their dogs for walks there. One time, this huge bulldog, about twenty inches tall, came tearing in and grabbed Prince by the neck. I just could not prise them apart. I hit the dog with everything I had, and if it wasn't for the fact that Prince had such long hair, the other dog would have killed him. In the end, it was my son Rory who managed to get them apart. What a relief that was.

Prince all but saved my life one time – or at least saved me from a beating – I'll be talking about that in the next chapter.

Chapter 12
The Club

My father was a member of the Workman's Club in Inchicore. He used to go down there regularly when I was a kid, to play billiards or read the paper, have a drink and chat to his mates from the war. That club played a very important role in the community. It was where the retired and unemployed men of the area went during the day. Open from ten in the morning to twelve or one at night, this was a big place – three floors. You could fit three hundred into the lounge easy. There was a bar as well and billiard tables. Newspapers were bought every morning. You could drop in there for a cup of tea and a chat with whoever was around.

Because Da had been a member, I joined just as soon as I was able. I used to use his cue playing snooker. All the old men had cues in little cases. Each one had a padlock on it, and the cases themselves had a special shelf in the club where they were kept. Everybody knew everybody else's cue.

When I joined the committee, the place was on its knees really. It had become a bit of a dump; it had those old tubular steel tables and chairs, with dirty, dark green upholstery. That wasn't the worst of it. The finances were in a state. The secretary at the time wasn't much use to be honest.

The first thing I did was introduce Bingo. There was no Bingo around the place at the time, but it had been big in England. This turned out to be a great success. We ran it on a Sunday and it raked in the money. We replaced the old furniture and brightened the place up a bit. There were a few unnecessary purchases but anyway.

That secretary died and we had a new set of executives. If anything, the new secretary was worse. He was a real holy Joe and would drop to his knees and call on the Blessed Virgin Mary at the drop of a hat. He prided himself on the fact that he never drank or smoked in his life, but he was a gambler, and he was bully. As soon as he and the new chair took over, the finances took another dive.

The members owned the club and the license that went with it. The building itself however was owned by shareholders. The club paid them a rent, but this was a nominal figure. I found out that the chairman was a shareholder, and I realised that this was a big conflict of interest. I could see too that the way things were going, if we didn't change how the club was run, it wouldn't be around for much longer. By the time the AGM came up, we were nearly eighty grand in the red. There was all kinds of skullduggery going on and the place was haemorrhaging money.

Just before the AGM was about to kick off, I went up to the chairman and asked if I could address the membership. 'Go ahead Rory,' he said. The place was packed.

'Gentlemen,' I said, 'my name is Rory and you all know me, and those that didn't know me before, you know me now. The club needs a tenner each just to keep the doors open. Why? Because none of our suppliers will give us credit. Why? Because we're not paying our bills. The chairman is about to tell you not to pay the ten pound to keep the club afloat. To those that don't know why, I'll tell you why. Because the chairman is a shareholder and if the club fails, the shareholders can sell the building and we'll have nothing. I propose that we remove the chairman from the chair and let the vice chair take the meeting.'

There was a big roar of approval. I had already put my name down as a candidate to be chairman. I was proposed and seconded, and no one would go against me, so now I was chairman, and I could get the old place back on track again.

As I say, the finances were so bad that we couldn't buy beer. I used to have to go down to Guinness's in the works van and pay for the beer out of my own money. At the time, I had a little engineering business and did work for all of the other clubs around the place – installing security gates and that. I used to go to them and they'd lend me a barrel of Harp or a barrel of Guinness.

The place was back on its feet in a couple of months. Suppliers were happy to extend credit to us again, and we no longer needed additional funds from the membership.

We used to run a Monday Club for fellas that didn't have very much. We'd get a few sliced pans, a pile of chips, some black and white pudding and take the lot of it into the snooker room. We'd have our feast while holding a singing competition. One side of the room against the other. And because we were a club, not a pub, we had the cheapest beer in Dublin.

We organised trips away. I'd have to hire eleven busses to ferry all the people that wanted to go: out to Ballbriggan, up to Termonfeckin, or as far away as Athlone. At closing time in Athlone, they'd leave us in a small bar on our own, and when everyone else was gone home, they'd open the place up and we'd have the run of the whole hotel. It was great.

I remember one time, we drank every pub in Ballbriggan dry of Guinness.

'Let us know when you're coming back,' they said, 'we'll have pigs' feet and ribs for all of yiz.'

We always made sure that everyone behaved themselves on these trips. If you acted up, you were barred the same as you'd be if you acted up at home.

The roof was the same one that had gone on a hundred years earlier when the place was being built, and it hadn't really been maintained

– there were leaks here and there. The shareholders couldn't afford to fix it, so I went to them and said that the membership would fund the works and they were happy with that.

I remember there was a carpenter on the committee. He offered to do the job for £25,000. Twenty-five grand? This was over forty-five years ago. You could have nearly rebuilt the place for twenty-five grand. Instead I did it by the book. I put it out to tender and got fellas to price materials and labour and the rest of it. Got the whole thing done for eight thousand. The old rafters were sound, but bowed, so the roofer braced them with new rafters, and I put in false ceilings and insulation everywhere, because the club could be freezing in winter. I also laid Axminster carpet upstairs and got some new furniture. I put in a new bar, which I designed myself, and got the fella who won apprentice of the year to do the bricklaying. I put in new toilets for the women downstairs – they used to have to climb two flights of stairs to get to the toilet, and I put in a new security system with cameras and buzzers. There'd always been a problem with what you'd call a criminal element in Inchicore. They'd intimidate the man on the door. This new system solved the problem for a while, but only for a while, because during my time in the club, that criminal problem got worse.

I was taking Prince for a walk up the canal one time when I was confronted by this fella I wouldn't let into the club.

'I'm going to fuckin' get you McClelland!'

Shit, I thought, I've my hands full here. He came on, shouting and threatening all kinds of things.

Next thing, Prince jumps out in front of me, stooped down low to the ground and started growling. I'd never seen him do anything like that before. In fact, I'd never even seen his back teeth before. I couldn't get over how long and white they were.

'Get that fuckin' dog away from me,' says your man.

'You fuck off,' I said, 'and the dog won't touch you.'

He lingered there for half a minute, but Prince looked so vicious, he wouldn't chance it, so he turned on his heel and walked off.

I arrived into the club one Saturday morning they told me that there was a guy at the bar, bollixed drunk and causing trouble. He shouldn't have been allowed in – he wasn't a member – and if you weren't a member, you had to be signed in by someone who was. But this was a big, intimidating guy; it would have been hard to refuse him anything.

He was so drunk that he was after pissing on the new carpet.

I went up to him and asked him to leave.

'No.'

'I'll have to get the police so.'

'Get them if you want.'

I called them and two cops arrived at the door. They both knew this guy well. One of them said to me, 'Go tell the barman to give him back his money, then take his pint.'

They followed me into the bar, I did as they asked, and then the bigger of the two cops said, 'Right, get out.'

He still wouldn't go, so the two coppers laid into him and gave him a right few clatters, then picked him up and carried him out of the place.

I wasn't long after buying a house in Inchicore, and these run-ins with criminals were worrying the kids. 'Da, we can't sleep. They'll kill you.'

That's why I resigned. I'd been chairman for four years, and when I left, there was £80,000 in the bank.

Chapter 13
Free Enterprise

After three years, I started to get sick of the docks. It was cold and dangerous and hard work. I had a notion of working for myself. I thought if I bought a minibus, I could generate enough cash to keep me going. So I found one and bought it, and started ferrying people around in the evenings after work. When it broke down, I had to ask Ted for the forty pounds to get it fixed.

'Forty?' said Ted, horrified.

He was a very decent man, Ted. No matter how much he protested, he'd never see you stuck. As he handed over the money he said, 'I haven't another penny, Rory. That's my last penny.' But then he always said that, and I always paid him back.

I had a bit of crack in the minibus with the kids. The engine was in the back, with a seat over it. I'd have them sitting there, then, going around corners, I'd wait till the last minute, lock hard and they'd go flying.

Robert was mad about horses. He had a horse up in the Dublin mountains, but one winter we got a bad snow, and he was out of his mind with worry about this horse. I'd a tow-bar on the minibus, so I borrowed a horsebox from a friend of mine, we all piled in and headed for the hills, stopping along the way to get a couple of bales of hay and a bag of carrots. But conditions got worse and worse the higher we got. Snow was coming down heavily – you could see it drifting against the ditches in the fields we passed, and of course the roads were in a bad way. At one point, I thought about turning back, but as I say, Robert was awful bothered about the horse. I had to keep going, but my heart was in my mouth – we were skidding were all over the road. We made it there safely and the horse was grand, not a bother on him. He was glad of the carrots though.

Later on, I rented a stable from a guy who owned a pub in Ballyfermot, so it was much easier for Robert to see the animal. Eventually, the horse got properly sick. He lay down and wouldn't get up, so I got a vet out to look at him. The vet shook his head and said that it was time to put him down. Robert was very upset, but I explained that these things happened.

Afterwards, we were all back in the house, waiting for the fella to come and collect the horse, and the vet starts making jokes about the dead animal. I had to tell the ignorant prick to keep his mouth shut in front of the kid.

Anyway, I couldn't make enough money out of the minibus, so I sold it and bought a lorry instead. And I decided to quit the docks and throw myself into this new venture. I knew a lot of people in the paper industry from my time in CB Sacks – I knew a lot of people all around Inchicore, Bluebell, Ballyfermot and beyond. I started by collecting up waste cardboard and paper and selling it onto the paper mills. This worked out really well. I'd buy up damaged reels of paper and haul them back to Clondalkin or even up as far as Portmarnock. There was a place in town that used hundreds of boxes a day. I did a deal with them that I'd take all of this packaging off their hands. I was recycling before recycling was thought of – old rolls of wallpaper, computer cards, all kinds of cardboard – you name it.

The way it worked in these places, you'd get weighed on the way in, then you'd unload and it was back onto the weighbridge to be weighed out. So I started carrying a big empty barrel in the back of the lorry and put a little tap on the bottom of it. I'd fill it with water before I went in with the load of paper, then, after I got weighed, I'd unload the paper, park up and let all the water out before weighing out again. Never got caught.

But hauling paper was often wet, dirty, difficult work. The damaged reels that I used to haul might have been lying around in the rain for ages, and would be dirty and smelly and soaking wet. I remember one night, the lorry broke down at traffic lights in Coolock and it took me half an hour of crawling around underneath before I managed to get it going again.

I was down in Rochfortbridge one afternoon, collecting a load of paper when I saw a Portakabin with a 'For Sale' sign on it. I parked up the lorry and went to take a look. It was basically a fully-equipped takeaway. There was a counter running the length of it, a place for patrons to come in and out and all the equipment you needed for making chips and burgers, grilling chickens and the rest of it. 'I'll fuckin' buy this,' I said to myself, so I made enquiries in the pub next door, found the man who owned it and did a deal. I had to hire a crane to get it on the back of the lorry, and then to unload it again in Camac park. The John F Kennedy Industrial Estate was after springing up behind our old house – in the field where I used to rob the milk – and there was nothing but a chain-link fence separating it from our garden. I got the crane to drop the Portakabin just inside the fence at the bottom of our garden. Then I made an entrance into the garden from the estate – which I know you weren't really supposed to do, but I needed a way for the hungry punters of Bluebell to get into our new takeaway. I got a load of flyers made up and went around the houses introducing myself. We took orders over the phone and delivered free to the area.

It went great at the start. We had queues of people coming in to get fish and chips and chicken and chips. But my wife insisted on working in the place, and she used to snipe at me all the time. I'd be talking to a customer and she'd say, 'Don't mind him being nice, he's a bastard.' That kind of thing puts people off, and after a while, business started to dry up. I put the Portakabin back on the market and eventually got a buyer. Lost money on it, but sure that's the way. Nothing ventured, nothing gained.

I knew I could be a good salesman, so I approached these guys who made gates and offered to sell them for them. I did fairly well at it, but the business didn't take off as I'd hoped. I'd been expecting a bit of momentum to build – you know, you do a good job for someone, they tell someone else and you get a bit more work. Turned out that the new business I was generating was just going back to the two guys who were making the gates – I wasn't seeing any commission. But I came up with a little workaround that redirected the business back to me, and soon after that, another of the guys that worked there asked me if I'd be interested in going into business with him, making our own gates and selling them instead.

This turned out to be a great little venture. We had a workshop in Inchicore where we made gates and all sorts of other iron work. When word of mouth took off, we started doing great business.

Round about midnight one winter night, I was nearly home when a sergeant pulled me in. He leaned over the windscreen and saw I'd no tax. I tried to plead my case. 'I've six kids up there, Sergeant, it's hard to manage.' He kept writing, but I could see he was cold, so I said to him, 'Why don't you sit into the car, you'll be more comfortable.'

So he did. It was a bad night, and he was in no hurry to go back out in it, so we chatted away, and I ended up selling him gates for his house. He agreed to scratch the tax charge. That wasn't all. At the time, my young fella, Robert had got pulled up for having no tax or insurance on his Honda 50.

'I'll sort that out for you too,' he said.

I went round the following day to measure up for the gates. But there was a lot going on and I kept putting the sergeant and his gates on the long finger.

At the time, there was a steel place up in Fox and Geese where I used to buy raw materials. You'd go into the office and order what you wanted – five of this, eight of that and so on. Then he'd print off the docket and you'd bring it down to the yard where another guy would help you load up. Between the office and the yard, I'd take out a pen and draw in another number on the docket. So five lengths of steel became fifteen and eight became eighteen. I got away with this for a while, but there was one time, I asked for ten, and added another zero before I got to the yard, so that the docket suggested I'd paid for a hundred. This was probably a bridge too far, because when I got to the yard, the guy was surprised at the size of the order. He started loading up, then he says, 'I need to go up to the office for something, I'll be back in a minute.'

'Here,' I said, 'give me that docket. I need it for my VAT return.'

VAT? I'd never paid VAT in my life, but your man handed me the slip of paper and went on up to the office. I stuffed the thing in my shoe. Five minutes later, he came back with the guy from the office who asked me how much I'd paid for.

'Ten,' I said, letting on to be getting impatient. I turned to the yard man. 'Gimme the docket, gimme the bloody docket till I show him.' He started patting his pockets, trying to find it. He'd totally forgotten he'd given it to me. 'Come on!' I said, 'we'll get to the bottom of this.'

'God,' says your man, 'Where did I put it?'

I left with the ten, and I was slow about going back there again, because I knew I'd be caught. The next time I needed steel, I took someone else with me and got him to go on into the place on his own, while I waited a couple of hundred yards down the road. That's where I was – sitting on the wall like a culchie when who drove up only the sergeant I'd promised the gates to.

'Hello Rory.'

'Howaya Sergeant.'

'You never did that gate for me.'

'Oh I'm really sorry,' I said, 'I lost that business.'

I didn't like telling him lies, but I was that busy, I just never got round to it. I changed the car after that and he didn't bother me again.

It was around this time too that I started picking up bales of high quality cloth at auctions around Dublin. I had them cut into suit lengths.

I was chairman of the club at the time, so what I did was I went around to all the men I knew and sold most of them a suit length. At two pound ten shillings a go, it was an easy sell, plus I had mate who made suits, so I put all of them onto him. I was very careful about one thing. I never let on to any of my customers that I was selling to anyone else. As far as they were concerned, they were getting an exclusive deal. But of course when the annual dinner dance came round, the cat got out of the bag very bloody quickly. Half the fellas in the place were wearing the same suit.

Someone said, 'Rory's cavalry is here.'

I got some slagging over it.

I'd sell anything. I sold a wig to a woman in a pub one time. I used to sell eggs too. We were skint at the time, living hand to mouth. I'd buy the eggs wholesale from Cotters in Newbridge, then go round selling them to all of the small shops in town. Made quite a bit of money at that.

I tried my hand at building too. The comedian Brendan Grace had an uncle Ned who owned a pub right here in Ballyfermot. He was a real character. He used to stand up in the middle of the pub and call for quiet. 'Right! We're now going to have the daily raffle. First prize is a fine head of luscious green cabbage, and the second prize is a box of teabags.'

He was a sort of an innocent in one way, but I got on great with himself and his wife.

He lived right next door to the pub. I built a double garage onto their house, then a wall right around the back of the place. He was a bit nervy, Ned. I remember he got me to install a couple of letter-box-sized holes in the wall that he could stick a shotgun out of. At the time, he had someone else doing building work in another part of the site. Ned came out to me one morning and said, 'Rory, the garage is leaking.'

'What?'

He made out that the roof of the garage I'd built was letting in water. So I went in and took a look. Sure enough, the wall was wet. I couldn't believe it, because I was sure I had done a good job, and I was proud of my work. But when I looked a little closer, I realised that the water wasn't actually coming from the ceiling at all. Someone had just thrown water against the wall. When I pointed this out to Ned, he realised that this other guy he had working for him was the culprit. He was just trying to make me look bad. Ned apologised and brought me into the off-license that adjoined the pub where we opened a bottle of Jameson.

When I finished that work, I piled the planks that we'd used in the scaffolding in his backyard. A little later on, I was doing work on my own house in Inchicore, so I asked Ned if I could borrow them.

'No problem Rory.'

It was a week or more before I got round to picking them up. Now, the pub and the house were right next door to each other as I say, but you couldn't get into the backyard of the pub – where the planks were – from the front, so we climbed into the backyard and started throwing the planks over the wall into the back garden of the house so that we could load them into the van.

Next thing Ned comes running out into the pub yard with his shotgun. Before we could even react he had fired both barrels into the air. We dropped everything and jumped into the van. By the time we got to the front of the house, Ned had realised his error and come through the house. He had dropped the gun somewhere and was waving his arms.

'Jaysus Rory, I'm sorry!' he said, 'I didn't recognise ye!'

'Don't worry Ned. No harm done.'

We had a bit of a falling out one time. He was building a house down in Wicklow, and asked me to put steel guards on all the windows. As I say, he could be quite a nervy fella. I had them made and ready to go, but the builder hadn't finished all the windows, and I couldn't put them on until the windows were in, so I couldn't do the job. I talked to the builder and he was happy to fit them when the windows were done. But Ned wasn't happy with this.

'I want you to fit them Rory.'

'Ned, there's no use me sending two men all the way down to Wicklow for fifteen minutes' work.'

But he insisted, and deducted a hundred pounds from the price we'd agreed. I was disgusted and I wasn't shy about telling him.

'I thought you were an honourable man, Ned. But I'll tell you what, you keep that hundred pounds. You need it more than me. Buy yourself a box of lollipops.'

That hit home. Next morning, I had an envelope through the door with a cheque for a hundred pounds in it.

I got to know Brendan Grace afterwards too, and his parents. Nice people, easy people to get on with. Ned bought a pub for Brendan out in Rathcoole – The Blackchurch Inn – and asked me to put up railings around it. I'd be driving up to Rathcoole with Ned and he'd have the window of the car wide open and his foot to floor. You couldn't hear a thing over the sound of the wind, but he wouldn't drive any other way.

Round about this time, things weren't going great with Tommy – my partner in the steel business, which is why I decided to just set up on my own altogether. I left him all the stock and machinery that we had and I started again from scratch. That was probably the best thing I ever did, because I was my own boss, I didn't have to rely on anyone, and I could work for myself from the workshop I'd built in the house in Inchicore. That went great for a while – it was probably the best earner I ever had. But things were about to take a sudden, dramatic turn for the worse.

Chapter 14
Mac the Knife

I used to go see my mother every single day, whether she was in the hospital or at home. I remember when the dementia started to set in.

'Where were you?' she said, when I arrived in.

'I was in yesterday Ma.'

'You weren't.' She listed every single one of us, some living, some not, and said they'd all been in to see her. 'But you, ya little pup ya, wouldn't come to see me.'

She used to embarrass me sometimes. I remember one Sunday – I was in my mid thirties at the time – I arrived in after a haircut. The house was full, as it always was on Sundays, with people playing cards and kids running around.

'Who cut your lovely curls?' she says.

When she died, we were all broken hearted. Martha, who was a couple of years older than me, came home from England. We were inseparable as kids, so it was great at least to see her after so many years.

I'd let myself get heavy. Both of us had. I remember one Monday morning, we were waddling around the kitchen.

'You know what?' I said, 'We're like two pigs here.'

She didn't appreciate that but it was the truth. 'Come on,' I said, 'till we do something about it.'

I called up the Olympic Health and Fitness Club on Mary Street that afternoon. This was a gym where men went one day and women the next. I made an appointment for both of us – me one day, her the next. When the day came, I went down there and they showed me around, I paid fifty pound each – a lot of money – and they made up an individual training programme for each of us. I enjoyed it from day one, and I enjoyed it even more when the weight started to come off. I went from sixteen stone down to ten. I lost the big red face and the boozer's nose. In fact, I'd go so far as to say that I got my youth back. And I held onto it too. Ever since then I've looked after myself and stayed fit and trim. But herself never kept her appointment.

It wasn't an easy marriage. I was unfaithful. I drank too much. But I was always a good provider. No one ever went short. And she could be a very difficult person to live with. There was a streak of violence there. I could do nothing right. She threw me out more times than I can remember. Often over nothing at all. She'd just take a figary and say 'Get out.'

I never put up a fight. 'Ok so.'

I'd go and stay with one of my sisters – usually Lily. I'd show up in her house, she'd see the bag and laugh. 'Are you out on the gur again?'

'I am.'

The first time my wife stabbed me, we were still living in Ballyfermot. My friend the checker down at the docks was after passing on another bale of cloth. Mustard yellow. I had a beautiful suit made. Everybody loved it.

'You look very smart in that Rory.'

I arrived home one evening and as soon as I was through the door, she came at me with the knife. She was always strong, and fast. She got me right there, at the lapel of the suit. I went down like a sack of potatoes, with her on top of me. Our son Robert was there, and he pulled her off. My hand went to my chest, but the knife hadn't even got through the suit – this was good quality material – but it turned out that it was only a butter knife. There was no point on it. I went up to bed, I never even looked at it, but the next day, the place where the knife had struck was black and swollen. I shuddered to think what would have happened if she'd used a better knife.

Nothing was ever said about that attack. No, hang on, that's not right. She said to me a few times, 'I'll get you properly the next time.' But most of the time, we just carried on as if it never happened. This was probably a mistake.

I mentioned that when I was doing up the house in Inchicore, I'd built this annex at the back of the house, and finished the inside in red brick – it was really classy. I'd also bought a Panasonic TV and a video player. This wasn't long after video players came out. It was a great little set-up, we were all delighted with it.

I was sitting in there with Veronica, yapping and watching a movie. Then, around midnight, she said, 'I'm going to bed Da.'

I felt asleep on the couch, and woke up at around three, freezing cold. I pulled myself off the couch and was heading out through the kitchen when she spoke. Eileen. She was sitting in the kitchen.

'Where are you going?' she said.

'I'm going to bed.'

'Get out.'

I looked at her. 'It's the middle of the night.'

'Get out.'

'Ok, fine.' I dug in my pocket for my keys. No keys. At that time too, I used always have a lot of cash on me. I needed it for buying steel for the gates. But when I went looking for the money I thought I had in my pocket, it wasn't there.

'I need my keys,' I said.

'No, get out.'

'Well give us the price of a B&B at least.'

'You're getting nothing.'

'Well in that case, I'm going to bed.'

What I didn't know is that she had a knife concealed at her leg where she sat. This was not a butter knife either.

I turned to go up the stairs. I don't think I even heard her get up. I felt something like a punch into my side, just above my hip, and when I looked down, I could see her hand on the handle of the steak knife, but I couldn't see the blade, because the blade was inside me. She drew it out to stick it in again, but Robert was suddenly there and he pulled her off again.

The next thing I remember, I was lying on the floor at the foot of the stairs, surrounded by medics and police.

I heard a copper ask something like, 'Are you going to charge this woman?'

'I can't,' I said, 'I have six kids with her.'

That's all I remember until I woke up in hospital the next day. I was told that the surgeon had been working all night, trying to patch me up.

If you'll believe this, the first doctor that spoke to me told me that my wife had been on the phone, and wanted to know if she could come in and see me.

'Are you joking?' I said, 'she tried to kill me.'

'Yes, but she's still your wife.'

Jaysus.

I lay there for two days, barely able to move. My brothers and sisters came in to see me. Their advice was all the same. 'You'll have to leave her Rory. And not come back this time.'

The kids came in too. 'When are you coming home Da?'

'I won't be coming home.'

There were only four of them left in the house at the time. Martina had gone to Liverpool, Eileen to Germany. Veronica, the youngest, was sixteen. Soon after that, she left and went to live with Tina. The three boys – Rory, Robert and Vincent – were the last to go.

When I was well enough, I moved back to Camac Park where Anne now lived. She had eleven kids, so the house was always full, but she was good to me.

There was a certain amount of relief in knowing that I was finally free of Eileen. I'd never have to go back to her again.

I couldn't work of course. I was making gates at the time, but I'd lost a lot of blood and had no strength left. And of course leaving home meant leaving work too. My workshop was in the house in Inchicore. If I wasn't going back there – and I wasn't – that meant starting from scratch again, at forty-seven years old.

Chapter 15
Starting Over

My business was gone, which meant my money was gone, so I had to go on the dole. I was still physically weak from the injury – and now I think about it, I was probably a bit post-traumatic as well. I was very nervous of the wound. I had my hand over it all the time, especially when I went into the club. I was afraid someone would hit me, messing.

'Don't touch me, I've stitches!'

Anyway, that's where I was one night – in the club – when one my mates, Denis, approached me with an idea. 'Why don't we go to California?'

America. I'd never thought of America before, but I did think about it now. The kids were grown up, I'd nothing keeping me here, so I said, 'Yeah, why not?' But we couldn't go right away. Denis was in the middle of selling a business, so he suggested that while we were waiting, we could go to Blackpool of all places. He had a girlfriend over there who ran a hotel.

Back to Blackpool? Why not? I hadn't been there in years.

This time, I didn't abandon my coat in a toilet. And we flew over. So no seasickness, and no waiting for the cattle to disembark at Birkenhead.

The place hadn't really changed much to be honest. It was the same holiday town: the same hotels, the same beaches, the same stalls and all that. You could get full board in Denis's girlfriend's hotel for forty pound a week, which wasn't bad. The only trouble was that this only got you two meals a day – breakfast and dinner. You had to fend for yourself at lunchtime, and that forty pound ate up all my dole. Sometimes Denis would buy me an apple to keep me going, but by dinnertime, I'd be starving.

There was a Catholic Club in Blackpool. I signed up and that's where I did most of my socializing. The big attraction there was the company, and the fact that the beer was cheap. To be allowed in, you had to give them the name of your parish priest.

'Fr. Ryan,' I said, pulling a name out of my arse.

'Do you go to mass?'

'Oh yeah, all the time.'

I remember they wouldn't let Protestants join — which was ridiculous in my view. They'd only give them associate membership.

I made a lot of Jewish friends in Blackpool at that time too. Holidaymakers who'd be staying in the hotel. They all knew I was skint, so they'd often buy me a pint. It's a thirsty horse will refuse a bucket of water.

In particular, I remember this retired doctor. Another Jewish man. He was in his seventies, and he was a lovely fella. We used to sit in the bar telling each other stories. He went back home to Manchester after his holidays, and I missed him, but didn't he show up again a few days later. He told me that he said to himself, 'I'm sitting here with nobody to talk to. At least in the hotel I could chat to Rory.'

I never went to the Dorchester, never went to see if the Yoxhalls were still above the ground. I don't know why. Maybe I was a bit embarrassed to be back again in Blackpool without much to show for it. Maybe I thought, sure why would they want to see me?

And I became Rory McDarby again. I was worried that if someone put Rory McClelland's name into the system, a little red flag might pop up, telling them that a kid of the same name deserted the British Army twenty years earlier. Better safe than sorry. There was a young fella staying at same hotel who was from Northern Ireland. His name was Tommy. This was at the height of the Troubles. His brother had been shot dead in Belfast, so he'd gotten out. He needed to sign on, same as I did, but didn't want to give his real name either. The shooting had been all over the papers.

I went down to the dole office with him. 'You need to have your name ready when you go in,' I said, remembering my mate Terry and his bogus alias, F-F-Fred Shaw.

'That's ok,' said Tommy, 'I have it ready.'
'What is it?'
'Steve McQueen.'
'You can't use that!' I said, 'they'll know it's fake.'

Martina was living down in Liverpool at the time, so when I got my dole on a Thursday, I'd head down and stay with her and her husband, Paul, who was a nice young fella. They had one kid, Peter, and we had great crack running around together.

We weren't in Blackpool very long when I realised that Denis never had any intention of going to California. He came to Blackpool to be with the girlfriend, and only wanted a bit of company while he was there. I didn't mind to be honest. It suited me to be away. If Denis hadn't lured me to Blackpool, I probably wouldn't have left the pubs of Inchicore.

I was down in Tina's one Friday when the door opened and who comes in only my wife. I nearly died. I hadn't seen her since she stabbed me. Veronica was with her, and this man that I knew from the club. Yaf was his name.

'Jaysus,' I said, 'what are yis doing here?'

'We came to see you Da,' said Veronica. I gave her a hug and a kiss, it was great to see her, but my wife? Or Yaf? He worked with me in Dublin, and sometimes I'd have a pint with him, but he wasn't somebody I was particularly close to.

It was the day of the Grand National, I remember that. They were all heading out to the pub to watch the race, but my health was still dodgy, and I wasn't in the better of seeing Eileen, so I said that I'd go upstairs and have a lie down while they went out.

Eileen says, 'Yeah, you all go out, I'll stay here and mind Rory.'

Thankfully, they all came back from the pub quickly enough. They were worried, I think, by the stressful situation they'd left me in. Eileen and Veronica didn't stay long – they headed for Dublin the next day, but that wasn't end of it.

I was back in Dublin – briefly – a few months later to do a job for a friend of mine, and my wife got word that I was home. I got a call from Veronica: 'Ma wants to see you'.

'I'd love to see you Veronica, but I don't want to see your ma.'

In the end, I couldn't refuse my youngest daughter, so I arranged to meet her mother in Ward's pub. I asked Veronica to stay for the whole interview. Eileen wasn't happy about that; she tried to send her away. I had it set up so that Eileen'd be sitting across from me – I wanted to keep the table between us – but she wanted to sit beside me; she made out she couldn't hear me. I wouldn't let her. Christ, even thinking about it now, I get the shivers. I was terrified of her.

So back I went to Blackpool, and apart from the odd visit, I wasn't back in Dublin for the bones of seven years.

At the beginning, I stayed in the same hotel in Blackpool. That's where I met Maria. She was from Leeds, but was down there on holidays with her mother. We hit it off right from the beginning, and pretty soon I was going down to visit her regularly. She had been married and divorced twice at this stage, and had two sons – twins – Damien and Christopher, who were eighteen. She had a few other children around the place too, but they were a bit older. I remember, when I stayed with them in Leeds, Damien would invite his mates over and introduce me as his dad. He'd often bring me into town, but I used to have terrible trouble finding my way back home. In fact, I couldn't really go out without Damien or I'd get totally lost. After a while though, I realised that he was bringing me in circles, taking the long way everywhere, just to keep me dependent on him, the little bollix. But I liked Damien, he was a nice young fella.

Meanwhile, back in Blackpool, I got a job on the outskirts of town with these two brothers. Real smart-arses. I remember one Friday, the younger one said, 'You'll have to fight our Albert for your wages.'

I said, 'I'll tell you what I'll do for you. I'll fight you and Albert, and when I win, I want both your wages.'

He tried to laugh it off. 'I was only joking.'

'Don't fuckin' joke like that with me.'

But they were awful mean, those two. Albert gave me a lift home one night and wanted money for petrol.

I was making boxes for them – safety boxes for storing tools on a building site. I started off making two a day and they were quite happy with that. Then I was asked to make three. By then I knew the place and the process very well, so I ended up being able to make four a day. They were delighted with that, but when I asked for better wages, they refused. I might have been making good money, but I wasn't being paid what I was earning, so I told them I'd take my cards that Friday.

The next job I got wasn't a thousand miles away from what I was doing in Dublin. Making roller shutters and cylinders and things like that. The factory was badly kept – steel and other bits and pieces lying around on the floor, machines without guards – you'd never get away with it today. I offered to make guards for the machines and racks to store raw materials; there was good stuff being ruined when forklifts rolled over it. The boss was delighted with this and ended up putting me in charge of quality control. But there was this manager there who didn't like the fact that the boss took a shine to me. He was always passing remarks about the Irish, and more than once he messed up measurements and tried to blame me for it.

They asked myself and this Geordie lad to fit a cylinder for a client on the far side of London – the bones of 400 miles away. He was to do the driving, I was to do the fitting. When we stopped for a break on the way down, I had a couple of bottles of Special Brew. Your man didn't like this.

'You can't drink on the job.'

'I'm not driving,' I pointed out, 'you're driving and you're drinking too.'

And he was. He had a couple of cans of beer. 'But it's not Special Brew,' he said, 'that stuff is far too strong.'

'Don't you fuckin' tell me what to drink.'

We were supposed to stay overnight, but the Geordie was afraid that the girlfriend would go off with someone else while he was away. So he refused to stay over, and we turned around and drove all the way back the same day. It took hours and hours.

Afterwards, he reported me for drinking on the job, but like I say, the boss liked me and didn't take any action. But things got worse between me and that prick of a manager. One day, he had this bit of rubber and he'd written in numbers along the length of it – in no particular order.

'Look,' he said, 'this is Paddy's measuring tape.'

'I'm fuckin' smarter than you, you prick,' I said, 'you're only a plonker.'

He sacked me on the spot. I went to see if the boss cold do anything about it, and I found out then that the manager was also a shareholder, so that was that.

'Fair enough,' I said, 'give me my cards so.'

I was in need of a bit of a change anyway, so I moved down to Leeds with Maria. She was living in a back-to-back house in Beeston. You don't have back-to-backs over here, but basically, you're surrounded. There are separate houses adjoining the back and side walls so that you can only have windows and a door at the front of the house. The place was cramped and stuffy. You wouldn't want to be claustrophobic.

We weren't long in it before we managed to get a better flat in a place called Little London.

When I got to Leeds first, there was fuck all work to be had. I used to go out to Harehills and stand in line with anything up to three-hundred other men. Nearly fifty years old and I was in the hiring line, hoping someone would take me on to swing a pick or heft a shovel for the week. There was one crowd – Murphys – run by Cork men, who had the contract to look after most of the roadworks in the city. These two fellas would walk up and down the line with their hands behind their backs, scowling at you. They hated Jackeens – that's what they called Dubliners – but most mornings, one of them would eventually nod at me. 'Git in that van.'

We were treated like shite.

The gangers used to sell breakfasts out the back of the works van. They had a little Primus stove and they'd cook up a couple of rashers and a couple of eggs for a sandwich and sell them at two pound a go. It was steep for the little bit of food you got, but if you didn't buy off them, you wouldn't be in the good books, and you wouldn't know what they'd have you at during the day. Before I'd left Dublin, I was doing more sales than anything else. My hands were white. At the end of the first day in Leeds, my palms were red and raw and my fingers were covered in blisters.

We were working in a place out near Bradford called Wakefield, digging trenches for cables. Little London was on the opposite side of the town to Harehills. I had to take two busses to get out there in the morning. On the way home in the van in the evening, we'd pass through the centre of town, so I asked the driver to drop me off there, where it was only a walk home.

He didn't even look at me. 'I'll drop you where I picked you up.'

I couldn't believe the ignorance of it, but two could play at that game. I picked up a lump hammer and said, 'You'll drop me on the other side of these lights, or I'll drop you.'

I got fed up taking the two busses. I had to be up in the middle of the night to get out to Harehills on time. There was this garage not far from where we lived where you could pick up cars cheap. It was a dodgy spot. You could tell that the minute you went in. You wouldn't cross the lads who worked there.

There was this Renault 4L for only fifty quid. I knew I was taking a chance. Once you drove it off the lot, that was that, there were neither guarantees nor comebacks, but like I say, I needed wheels so I bought it and it ran fine for a while. I'd drop Maria to work, then I'd go on to work myself. Then one Sunday morning, myself and Maria were out and didn't the passenger door fall off. Just like that, as Tommy Cooper used to say. I pulled in the car – we were outside a pub called The Rifleman – went back, dragged the passenger door off the street and settled it in place. I had an old pair of work trousers in the back of the car. I tied one end to the door and the other to the divider in the backseat. Believe it or not, we went around like that for months.

Another morning, I was leaving Maria to work as usual, but there was this noise coming from the front of the car, the kind of noise you can only ignore for so long. I pulled in, got out, and found that the radiator was after slipping down and was scraping along the road. Shit, I thought, what am I going to do with this?

So Maria headed off to work on foot, I left the car there – it was outside the university – and took a bus home. I got a couple of wire coat-hangers and a few tools and went back to the car, jacked it up and tied the radiator onto the grill with the wire, then I took it back to the garage where I bought it. They weren't happy to see me.

'You bought the car sight unseen,' I was told, 'there's nothing I can do about it.'

'It goes great when it gets going,' I said, 'but it's just a bit slow to start in the morning.' I decided I wouldn't mention the trousers holding the door on, or the fact that the radiator would be on the road outside Leeds University if it wasn't for coat-hangers.

There was another car parked up in front of the office. A Volkswagen. 'How much do you want for that?'

He scratched his chin, then he says, 'Tell you what. Leave the Renault here, gimme twenty quid and you can take the VW.'

I didn't need to be asked twice. I gave him the twenty pound, hopped in the Volkswagen and got out of there fast.

I drove that car for years. I even took the ferry from Holyhead and drove it back to Ballyfermot.

Meanwhile, back in Harehills, I was getting sick of the back-breaking labour and mean oul bastards I was working for. You were on the sub all the time. They'd give you money out of your wages ahead of time, then on payday, they'd pay you the rest in the pub – for which they were getting backhanders off the publican.

They'd do everything in their power to avoid paying you. If you told them you were going to pack it in, they'd hold money back and tell you to come and pick it up another day. They relied on the fact that you'd have another job miles away and couldn't take time off to come out and collect what you'd earned. I wanted to leave, so I asked one of the foremen I'd made friends with what I could do to make sure I got my money. His advice was to 'sub up tight' – meaning, get as much as you possibly could ahead of payday so that you'd have so little owing that they wouldn't bother holding it back. But when I left for another job, they did end up keeping a chunk of my money. Bastards.

The next job I got was making cylinders in Forbes' Engineering. It was a hell of a lot easier than working on the roads, and the work itself was child's play compared to what I used to do in my workshop in Inchicore. There was no place to eat there, so I used to go up to the pub for lunch. No one ever challenged me on it, so my lunch hour started to get a bit longer, to the point where I'd take two hours every day. I remember the landlady had a vicious little bulldog. She'd have to hold it back to stop it from going for me. She gave me a dirty big wink one day and said, 'He's after your bollix same as I am, Rory.'

But the pay was poor for the quality of the work I was doing, which is why I continued to draw the dole and never gave Forbes's my cards. I told them I'd go on the books if I got more money, but they wouldn't give me any, so I left in the end.

After that, I rented a car and got a job as a hackney. Funny really. When I first came to Leeds, I couldn't find my way around on my own, but after a couple of years, I knew enough to go taxiing. You did have to do separate driving and knowledge tests to get in.

My driving examiner was this big English lad. He had a handlebar moustache. He kept calling me Paddy, which, as you may have noticed by now, I don't like.

'My name's not Paddy.'

'Sorry!' he said, 'force of habit.'

But he was a decent fella, and next thing he starts telling me jokes, and I started telling him jokes and at the end of it, he said, 'You passed with flying colours.'

The knowledge test was easy enough in those days – not half as difficult as it is in Dublin.

I worked for a company that operated out of Leeds market, which was enormous. There were twenty-four butchers' shops all together on the one row and they'd be all standing out at their doors shouting their wares.

Leeds wasn't the safest of cities in those days. Taxiing could be dangerous. There was one Irish fella who worked with me, he picked up a woman in town, and when they got to the destination, there was a gang of fellas waiting to beat the shite out of him and take his earnings.

There were riots in Chapeltown – a no-go part of the city – while I was there, and a lot of gang violence. I remember sheltering in a supermarket one night while there were running battles on the street outside. Some of Maria's sons got involved and things didn't go so well for them. The twins and the older son were arrested and given six month sentences. To make it worse, the bastards separated the twins and sent Damien to Durham, which was hundreds of miles away. The day we went to see him, we were on the road for hours and hours, and when we got there, visiting hours were over. In fairness to them, they let us in and we had a good visit. The other two went to Armley in Leeds and had a difficult time of it in there. Rotten place, Armley Prison.

I got a call one night from a pub I used to go to the odd time. The General. Albert was the name of the fare. I half knew Albert; everybody did. He was huge – six foot six, and a deaf mute. He had a fruit barrow in the market.

When I got to the pub, I found your man and signalled to him that I had the taxi ready outside, then went back out and sat into the driver's seat. While I was waiting, I talked to the controller on the radio. She asked me who I was picking up.

'Albert. The big guy with the fruit stall.'

'What?' she says, just as he's opening the door and sitting in. 'Don't take him! He never pays.'

'Now you tell me,' I said, 'he's in the cab. What'll I do?'

'Get the money off him before you start.'

So I started gesturing to him. 'Two pound, it'll be two pound.'

He looked at my hands and started shaking his head. No. He wasn't paying. I got back on to base. 'He won't pay me.'

'Then don't take him.'

There was a lot of gesturing back and forth, both of us getting more annoyed, until eventually he reached into his pocket and pulled out two pound.

But the trouble was only getting started. Even if you forgot the disability, Albert was very drunk and no matter what he did, I could not figure out where he wanted to go. I was driving around the centre of the city, he was gesturing and making noises and I was gesturing and making noises, but I hadn't a clue what he was getting at and he hadn't a clue what the fuck I was saying. I got it into my head that he wanted to go up by Armley Prison, so that's where we went. We were both pissed off by then, so when he started gesturing that he wanted to be let off outside this pub near the prison, I was more than happy to pull in.

Then he started looking for his money back.

'Fuck you,' I said, 'that's not happening.'

This started another row: him looking for the two pound, me telling him to get the fuck out of the car. He folded the arms and sat there.

'Right,' I said. I got out, went round to the back and opened the boot. Every car was required to have a fire extinguisher and this one was no different, so I picked it up, checked the instructions, pulled out the pin, opened the driver's door and I let him have it. I emptied the full canister of powder into the car, and I enjoyed every second of it.

Albert just sat there with his hands up, but now that I'd finished and the canister was empty, he opened the passenger door, dragged himself out and stood there, leaning on the car, completely covered, head to toe, in white powder. You could just see his two eyes and nothing else. But he wouldn't let go the door, so I came round and I punched him on the chin. He was so tall I had to jump up to do it. That rocked him, and he let go, so I closed the door, got back in at the driver's side, shut the door and tore off. The last I saw of him, he was striding across the road towards the pub, looking like the abominable snowman.

Now, I should say that this was a rented car. I don't think I'd have emptied a fire extinguisher into it if it had been mine – satisfying and all as it was. But the laughing when I got back to base. In fact, it was such a great story that the lads in the rental place weren't bothered by all the powder in the car. Everyone knew Albert was a bit of a bollix.

I was careful for a few weeks after that. The base was right beside where Albert worked, so if I got a fare there, I'd pick up at the backdoor instead.

Six weeks later, I walked into the pub where I'd picked him up with Maria. When she saw Albert towering over the bar, she grabbed my arm. 'Come on, let's get out of here.'

'No,' I said, as he clocked us, 'we'll drink a pint.'

He was scowling over at me while the pints were being pulled, and when the barman set them down on the bar, well, you never saw a woman down a pint as quick. But I took my time. We had our pints, and Albert did no more than scowl. For years afterwards, people'd be singing the theme from The Snowman at him. 'We're walking in the air!'

Anyway, after a few years, the relationship with Maria began to go south. We fought a lot, and in end, I decided it was time to leave and hit the road for Holyhead, A long oul drive when you're on your own, but that was the end of that.

It wasn't easy, coming back to nothing very much in Dublin. But I still had a lot of friends. I lived with my son Rory for a bit, then I got a place on my own and I went taxiing.

Chapter 16
Just Keep Swimming

My two favourite brothers were Gerry and Paddy. But Paddy was taken from us far too young. Cancer. He was only 47. When he was in hospital, I used to go see him every day, sometimes twice a day. He was a big man: about fifteen stone, but he was nicely built, he had the height to carry it. Towards the end, he went down to seven stone and was in terrible pain. I even thought about choking him, just to save him from it. He used to say, 'Roll, will you go down and ask the nurse for more morphine?'

So I'd go down, but they would only say, 'There's no point, he'll only vomit it back up again.'

Death, when it came, was a relief.

And then lightening struck again. My son Rory was taken from us at only 55. He was a real gentle soul, but at the same time a great laugh. Everyone loved him. People would say, 'I was talking to Rory the other day, he's a gas character.'

I'd be bursting with pride. But he had a heart attack and died and my heart broke. I didn't know how I was going to come back after that, but swimming helped a lot. At one point, I was swimming a full mile in the pool every day. These days, I'm down to a kilometre, but then there's not many eighty-four year olds capable of that. There's something about the water and the slow, repetitive rhythm of swimming that I find very therapeutic.

After I lost Rory, it was very hard to get up out of bed and do anything. These days, I remind myself. I'm alive. I got what Rory never had. I have no reason for complaint.

Back when I was drinking, I used to get this recurrent pain in around my kidneys. It was excruciating. I was in and out of hospitals and they could never get to the bottom of it, but I knew it was related to the drink because it would go any time I came off it. I couldn't pretend to myself that it was anything else.

I used to get a cough bottle and drink half of it straight down, just to be able to go to work. That made my face go like a beacon. Because of the pain, I'd go around with my hand held across my middle. They started calling me Napoleon in the club.

I suppose I drank to cope. I'm off it twenty years now. Believe it or not, once I made up my mind, I didn't find it hard to stop.

***

I was in a hotel in Leeds one time, I starting chatting to these two fellas. I can't remember what we were talking about, but one of them complemented me on the suit I was wearing.

The second man frowned. 'Yes,' he said, 'but the sleeves are too long.'

Those words had the strangest effect on me. I could almost feel something inside of me break. I don't know what look came over my face, but when they saw it, they both drew back. I'd frightened them.

I didn't say another word, I stood up and ran to the toilet. I tore open the cubicle and slammed and locked the door after me, then I sat down on the toilet and I broke down. For a full hour, all I could do was sob and sob and sob. It was as if there was a huge reservoir of sadness inside me, and those two lads – who I never saw again – they let it free. It was the best thing that ever happened to me. Afterwards, the relief!

There's something about clothes that goes very very deep with me. These days, I won't leave the flat unless I'm immaculately turned out. I have eleven different suits that I wear according to my mood. Sometimes a tie, sometimes a cravat. Nice shine on my shoes.

I suppose in many ways, I'm still the ragamuffin sitting on the kerb, afraid of how I'll be judged. I think that even after you escape poverty, you carry it around with you in ways no one else can see.

***

The fact that I'd gone AWOL from the British army bothered me for a long time. I was only a kid – I'd lied about my age to get in – but I was very proud of my father, and I didn't want to sully his name. So I decided that I'd do something about it.

I went down to the British Embassy on Merrion Road and presented myself to the man on the front desk. I'd told him I'd gone AWOL in

1957. He told me to take a seat and went to get someone else. It was a nervous wait. I had visions of being dragged back to England and thrown into the military prison in Colchester. And I'd seen how they'd treated deserters when I was stationed in Winchester. But I'd made my mind up to face the music, whatever it would be.

A man in uniform came out and I gave him my number – 23545221. I'd never forgotten it, not least because I learned that if you did forget it, you got the butt of a rifle into the chin.

He shook my hand and I explained the whole thing to him. He put my worries to bed fairly quickly, and two weeks later I got letter in the post:

'I am writing in reply to your approach to the British Embassy in Dublin regarding your wish to terminate your Illegal Absence from the British Army.

In view of the fact that you have now reported to this Directorate, it has been decided that you are no longer required for Army Service and disciplinary proceedings will not be taken against you.'

The best part of it was that they gave me a pension of twenty pound a week!

***

There have been many great moments. I taxied for years and years in Dublin, and I made a many great friends. I'm respected around here, and that's important.

I remember I came back to Ballyfermot with Maria about six or seven years after I'd given up the chairmanship of the club. They'd organised a dance, but it wasn't in our club – we never had a dance license and always had to rely on a neighbouring club when we wanted to put one on. I didn't go in – we didn't have tickets – so we were having a drink in the bar instead. I looked up as one of the members passed by on the way out of the dancehall.

'Rory! Is that you?'

He came over and shook my hand and we had a bit of a chat. Then he went back into the dance. Shortly after that, the music stopped and next thing the bar flooded with people, and a queue of couples formed at the table to shake my hand. Well, that was a proud moment, one that I never expected.

It's a nice thing to be remembered for the good you've done.

Printed in Great Britain
by Amazon

59268901R00119